THE BIBLE YOU DON'T GET IN CHURCH

The Pathway to a New Revelation

If you know the truth, it will set you free.

Lewis Tagliaferre

To Norma, Blessings & memories

Lewis Tagliaferre

ISBN 978-1-64492-020-6 (paperback)
ISBN 978-1-64492-021-3 (digital)

Copyright © 2019 by Lewis Tagliaferre

All rights reserved. No part of this publication may be reproduced, distributed, or transmitted in any form or by any means, including photocopying, recording, or other electronic or mechanical methods without the prior written permission of the publisher. For permission requests, solicit the publisher via the address below.

Christian Faith Publishing, Inc.
832 Park Avenue
Meadville, PA 16335
www.christianfaithpublishing.com

Printed in the United States of America

CONTENTS

Preface 5
Acknowledgments 9
Introduction 11
The Bible Story 17
    History of the Bible 17
    In the Beginning 25
    Chosen Fathers and Mothers 28
    Slavery, Exodus, and Covenant 30
Settlement in the Promised Land 33
The Kings and Prophets 35
    Kings 35
    Leaders of God's People 38
Exile and After 40
Other Writings in the Old Testament 43
Between the Testaments: 400 BCE to Jesus 45
Jesus and the Kingdom of God: BCE–30 CE 49
The Early Church: 30–60 CE 66
The Letters of Apostle Paul: 48–62 CE 70
Other New Testament Letters 76
The Revelation to John 79
Commentary 80
    The Old Testament 83
    The New Covenant 93

    The Sinful Nature of Mankind 97
    Eternal Punishment 100
    Jesus as Messiah 104
    The Plan of Salvation 106
    Discussion of the Afterlife 113
    The Incipient Church of Christ 122
    The Gospel According to Paul 134
    Reconciling Jehovah and God 155
    Eschatology 161
A New Pathway to Enlightenment 167
    Growing Beyond the Bible 170
    A New Revelation 176
    Final Steps 185

Appendix A: Commandments Of Jesus 195
Appendix B: Instructions of Apostle Paul 205
Appendix C: The Nicene Creed 210
Appendix D: How the Myers-Briggs Type Indicator
Applies to Christian Faith 212
Appendix E: My Favorite Hymn 218
Recommended Resources 221

Preface

I deem those blessed to whom, by favor of the gods, it has been granted either to do what is worth writing of, or to write what is worth reading.

—Pliny the Younger

I confess to being one of those Christians who relied upon the official publications of my church leaders while I was a Sunday school teacher and deacon. When my wife died at age fifty-two, neither the pastor nor any church members could help me survive the horrible grief. If God is all-loving and omnipotent, how come suffering is so ubiquitous among his creation? After untimely death of his beloved wife, British writer and Christian apologist C. S. Lewis (1898–1963) lamented that when he needed the help of God to survive, the door of grace seemed to be closed, locked, and barred on the other side; the lights were out; and no one seemed to be present. He died of a broken heart soon after he wrote *A Grief Observed* (*1963*) in which he declared, "No one told me that grief feels so much like fear." Lewis summarized the problem of pain and grief thus: "If God were good, he would make his creatures perfectly happy, and if he were almighty he would be able to do what he wished. But the creatures are not happy and tortures occur, so they must be necessary. Therefore, God lacks either goodness, or power, or both… There is not much chance I will stop believing in God. What I fear is coming to believe such terrible things about him. So, this is what God really is like; deceive yourself no longer." Scripture says it is a dreadful/fearful/terrifying thing to fall into the hands of the living God. It is even more terrifying to see him as he really is. (Hebrews 10:31)

Since I found no comfort in my church, I began a search of the Bible to keep me alive and working during my grief. After I looked into it, I found virtually that all the official literature and teaching aids were "proof texts" carefully chosen (a.k.a. cherry-picked) to highlight the learning/teaching objective for indoctrination while the full story was left undisclosed. It was only after I began to look beyond the official published proof texts that I became interested in what the Bible actually says. With the aid of a *Thompson Chain Reference Bible*—possibly the best Bible resource ever published—I was able to trace topics linked throughout scriptures instead of concentrating on books, chapters, and verses as most theologians do. The latest edition provides linked reference guides for more than 8,000 topical studies. With this resource, researchers can find connections between scriptures that otherwise would never be detected, thus seeing the Bible through different eyes instead of the normal book, chapter, and verse reading that results in proof texting.

As I researched biblical topics for myself, I found new information right there in front of me on the printed pages that reshaped my opinion and sent me in a whole direction. Perhaps proof texting (a.k.a. cherry-picking) scriptures is necessary to avoid disclosing the truth, which might destroy the basic foundations of the Church and leave Christians with no firm ground on which to stand. I think over-generalizing from a specific scripture—that is, assuming a scripture intended for its time and place is meant for everyone, everywhere all the time—is the greatest error of Bible interpretation. Avoiding the truth only makes it more shocking upon final discovery—like when you find out Santa Claus is more of a symbol than a reality, but a necessary symbol nevertheless. Similarly, the whole Jesus thing may be a symbol of some eternal reality much larger than the symbol itself. To focus on the symbol is to miss the larger reality, which extends beyond the Bible to a new revelation.

So I began to compile a personal journal of the Bible story, as in "the Bible says," not as some scholars' or churches' interpretations since I am neither a scholar nor church leader, but only as an interested layman taking it as it is published in modern English. After more than thirty years and nearing the end of my life at age eighty-five, this is the result, consolidated and organized for easy reading. This is not what theologians or philosophers say about it; this is what the Bible itself says. I think it is a way of telling the stories in the Bible differently from most other sources, and one that you may find interesting and helpful in your spiritual growth. I am not trying to convince you of anything. I am just presenting the scriptures possibly in a different way than you have read or heard in the past. Proof texting the Bible is dangerous. But the truth can be liberating.

My extensive study of the Bible raised many questions and exposed many conflicts, so I needed a new belief system I could die with. After much research, meditation, and therapy, I found my solution. I call it theofatalism (a.k.a. theological determinism.) Of course, you can draw your own conclusions and apply your own interpretations just like everyone does. No book is perfect, so you can add your own comments and notes to improve it and post your opinion on this book page on www.amazon.com. All in God's will of course. Thank you.

Acknowledgments

I am grateful to Adam Mellott and his team at Christian Faith Publishing for their work in making my book available to the public and for giving it their professional touch. The Bible Story section is derived primarily from a work titled "A Short History of the Bible" posted on the Internet in 1997 written by Burton G. Yost, Professor Emeritus of Bible and Religion at Bluffton College(1961–1993) and Loren L. Johns, PhD, Professor of New Testament, Anabaptist Mennonite Biblical Seminary. It is reprinted with edits and supplements by permission under fair use doctrine for education and discussion purposes. Additional resources used in the commentary came from many sites on the Internet, principally discussions posted to Wikipedia. Bible quotes use the New International Version posted on www.biblegateway.com with permission. Authors of the referenced books and Web site hosts are much appreciated for adding their research to my understanding. However, the positions expressed herein are my own and do not imply endorsement by any of the contributors. This discussion is not intended as an academic work of scholarship, but rather as a personal layman's commentary. It is based on several decades of reading the Bible and my church attendance while serving as a deacon and Sunday school teacher, followed by many years of personal contemplation and study. I also appreciate any and all those who read this material and find it useful in their personal growth.

INTRODUCTION

Unless I am convinced by the testimony of the scriptures or by clear reason, I am bound by the scriptures I have quoted, and my conscience is captive to the Word of God.

—Martin Luther

All scripture is given by inspiration of God, and is profitable for doctrine, for reproof, for correction, for instruction in righteousness.

—2 Timothy 3:16

You shall know the truth and the truth will set you free.

—John 8:32

You can't handle the truth.

—Col. Nathan R. Jessup,
A Few Good Men, 1992

The Holy Bible is the most popular book in the world, with more than 2 billion people claiming to be its adherents and 100 million copies sold every year. Most Christians, if not all, probably possess at least one copy. However, it is unlikely that owning a Bible assures that it is openly discussed or even read, except by scholars and theologians. The Bible has been described as "the most popular book never read." Most Christians rely on what they get in Sunday school and church services, concentrating on the topics presented by authorities in their respective hierarchies as scheduled annually by the established lectionaries. Opinions about its historicity and interpretations vary immensely, even among scholars, and new ones are being published continuously. So it is understandable that most Christians never really read it for themselves and merely absorb what they get from their church leaders. Maybe they are too busy, or maybe they are afraid of what they might learn, or maybe it is too confusing—or maybe it is the will of God. After all, God is not an idea you want to treat lightly, so it could be safer to leave discussing it up to the experts. If you screw up, it could be very painful for all eternity. Nevertheless, opinions about the Bible vary immensely. The basic question readers of the Bible must ask themselves is, "What has that got to do with me?"

Dr. Loren L. Johns explained various related views on its divine inspiration:

- The view of the Bible as the inspired word of God: the belief that God, through the Holy Spirit, intervened and influenced the words, message, and collation of the Bible
- The view that the Bible is infallible and incapable of error in matters of faith and practice, but not necessarily in historic or scientific matters
- The view that the Bible represents the inerrant Word of God, without error in any aspect, spoken by God and written down in its perfect form by humans uniquely selected as scribes

Within these broad beliefs many schools of interpretation operate. Progressive Bible scholars claim that discussions about the Bible must be put into its context within church history and then into the context of contemporary culture of its time to be applied properly to modern times. For them, the Bible merely is a starting point for a venture into theology driven to wherever one is led by the Holy Spirit, and each one is a priest unto themselves in their time and place. Purists say one cannot really understand the Bible unless you read it in the ancient Greek and Hebrew languages. Fundamentalist

Christians often claim the doctrine of biblical literalism, where the Bible is not only inerrant, but the meaning of the text is also clear to the average reader. "The Bible says it, I believe it, and that settles it." After all, one may ask if you cannot take it literally in your own modern language, why take it at all? It seems to be much more complicated than that when you really look into it. There is scarcely any contention that cannot be supported with a little effort by proof texting, (a.k.a. cherry-picking) scripture to prove a point.

I tend to be more realistic with a need for scriptures to make sense for us today, if that is possible. Unfortunately, it seems the gap between literal fundamentalists and progressives is growing wider within Christianity. Progressives might say the Bible must be taken as a living book and interpreted in light of modern culture. For example, at the "last supper," Jesus broke bread and told his apostles, "Take eat, this is my body" (Matthew 26:26). Was he condoning cannibalism? Was it mere symbolism, or did the bread magically become his body and does so during the Mass after consecration by the priest as claimed in the Catholic catechism? Why do so many Catholics think it is true? St. Augustine of Hippo (354–430 CE) upheld the early Christian understanding of the real presence of Christ in the Eucharist, saying that Christ's statement "This is my body" referred to the bread he held in his hands and that Christians must have faith that the bread and wine are in fact the body and blood of Christ, despite what they see with their eyes.

Apologetics pass off such questions merely as a "mystery," and many people accept them as such. Progressives, like Bishop John Spong, might suggest such scriptures are too fantastic to be acceptable in modern churches. He claims he can disbelieve the virgin birth, the miracles, and the resurrection and still be a Christian. Bishop Spong writes that such unbelievable accounts in the Bible must be stripped away to get into the core gospel of Jesus, which leaves little firm ground for the fundamentalists to stand upon (*Unbelievable,* 2018). Spong is reviled and condemned as leaving the Church while still declaring himself a Christian.

Similarly, Thomas Paine (1737–1809), a father of the American Revolution and passionate advocate for human freedom, wrote,

"All national institutions of churches, whether Jewish, Christian or Turkish, appear to me no other than human inventions, set up to terrify and enslave mankind, and monopolize power and profit… I do not mean by this declaration to condemn those who believe otherwise; they have the same right to their belief as I have to mine. But it is necessary to the happiness of man that he be mentally faithful to himself." He urged his readers to employ reason instead of fear in forming their religious beliefs (*Age of Reason*, 1807, 2015). Paine also was reviled and exiled for deconstructing the Bible by the same political leaders who had honored him for helping them engage the American public in the revolution. Someone said it is dangerous to attack established institutions, especially religious ones with 2,000 years of tradition and vast international resources with many vested interests. In following Paine, Thomas Jefferson edited his own version of the Bible by cutting out all the miracles and pasting up his abbreviated version. In contrast, this work presents the Bible as it is with no editing or proof texting.

Some theologians claim that the Bible must be interpreted in the context of its time and place, so selectively applying scriptures to current times and places is a form of proof texting (a.k.a. cherry-picking) that produces false conclusions. The Bible warns several times of false prophets who would deceive even the very elect—ten times in the Old Testament and seven times in the New Testament. True or false may not be the appropriate dichotomy. Perhaps its relevance or nonrelevance or usefulness is a more appropriate basis for applying scriptures to modern times. Is there a role for the Bible in modern times, and if so, what is it? Poet Robert Frost (1874–1963) wrote, "Lord, please forgive my many little jokes on thee and I will forgive thy great big one on me." He lost his wife and five of six children by age sixty-two, and then he lived until age eighty-eight to think about it. He concluded, "It is hard to get into this world and hard to get out, and what lies in between makes no sense." One may ask, where is God in all this suffering? The answer is the same place he was when his only son was being crucified on the cross. So if you try to make any sense of it all, forget it and go outside and play. It was with that degree of skepticism about organized churches and their dogma that

I began to read the Bible for myself, not for its implications or context, but for its content alone. It is an interesting read, if nothing else. But for many, it is something far more than mere literature.

Empires have come and gone during the evolution of the Bible, but it has endured past all of them. The miracle of the Bible is not so much what it says or where it came from as the fact that it has survived for more than two thousand years, and millions of people annually are added to the flock of its adherents from wide-ranging cultures around the world. Whether it is fact or fiction, nobody really knows for sure. Some of it seems to be anchored in history and other parts merely extensions of myth and legend. How can one ancient book containing so many ridiculous stories appeal to so many diverse people for so long unless there is some force beyond human understanding that makes it continue? The stories in it are so flawed by human standards of logic and reason that in any other book genre, it would be classified as fiction or, at best, merely legend and mythology. The difference between reality and fiction is that fiction must make sense. The Bible fails to meet even that criteria. Nevertheless, there is an endless stream of preachers, writers, and publishers who regale their flocks with its many stories and implicitly or explicitly imply through continuing proof texting that there is something in there for modern people to learn and apply to life if only they could figure out what that is. Each one has their own interpretation, and each generation of readers searches for its meaning to them. The same goes for me too and perhaps for you also.

This book begins with a history of the Bible and proceeds from there to a personal commentary that compares and contrasts many scriptures that seem to confuse and frustrate instead of enlightening and comforting readers who take them literally. After the history, the commentary discusses selected themes in scriptures, letting them speak for themselves in relation to the basic dogma of Christian theology. This is not the Bible proof texted to prove a dogma as you likely get in church or Sunday school. It is what it is and says what it says.

Deconstructing the Bible is easy, but it is not so easy to find the way beyond conflicting scriptures into a new interpretation that accommodates reality as it really is. The pathway to a new revelation attempts to reconcile the reality of scriptures with a broader belief system that can accommodate all the holy books and all the many world religions. This conclusion points to a GOD above gods, one that is the primary source of all that happens in the universe from atoms to galaxies and possibly beyond. This belief requires a giant leap of imagination into a realm of intuition and energetic spirit that only a few readers may be able to accept. Many people reach a plateau early in life from their church experience and remain there all their lives. Some see things as they are and ask why. But others see things that could be and ask, why not? Others cannot seem to change unless it hurts too much not to. All in God's will, of course, as there can be no other. In my opinion.

> The universe is a very big place, so its long distances in space are measured by how far light travels in a year at the speed of 186,000 per second. That is a very big number. The farthest stars detectable are estimated to be about 13.9 billion light-years from earth, and they are speeding away at ever-increasing rates, making it appear that space itself is expanding. Since the stars we see at night actually are the tips of light beams that left many light-years ago, we are looking at the history of their existence. Each spot of light is a galaxy containing many billions of stars like the sun that powers our planet earth. It is but one star among billions in the galaxy called the "Milky Way" for its appearance at night. The earth is one of eight planets circulating in very precise and dependable orbits around the sun. Any slight variation in its orbit, and life on earth could not exist as it does. Science, working backward, assumes the universe came from an original event that created all matter from nothing called the "Big Bang." The science of cosmology encounters more mysteries the more it discovers about the cosmos.

The Bible Story

History of the Bible

The Bible is a collection of books that make up the sacred scriptures of the Christian and Jewish faiths. The Bible was written by many different and disconnected authors spanning more than one thousand years. The earliest writings are thought to have been written in Hebrew, Aramaic, and Greek. There are eighty books in the King James Bible—thirty-nine in the Old Testament, fourteen in the Apocrypha, and twenty-seven in the New Testament. Most modern Protestant editions omit the Apocrypha, which is included in the Catholic Bible; in those editions, the number of books totals sixty-six. The Jewish scriptures, called the Tanak, contain the same books as the Protestant Old Testament, except that the books are combined and arranged in a different order. The first five books, called the Torah, provide the main scriptures of Judaism. Each of these three collections is called the "canon," that is, the official scriptures of that group.

More important than the list or the number of writings is what followers think they contain. Christians and Jews say that the scriptures are the record of God's eternal word or message about God and his relation to humankind and the created world. Most of this message takes the form of history of a small band of people called Hebrews because it is understood that the Lord God revealed himself through entering and acting in their lives and has guided the interpretation of those deeds for the rest of humankind. This story of God's words and deeds as understood by his chosen people forms the main structure of the Bible. In addition to the main story, there are other writings: religious poetry and prayers, wise sayings, and explorations of human wisdom. These other writings also relate to the basic story of God and his purposes.

The original story of Jesus, who never wrote anything himself, was distributed orally for several decades before the first manuscripts were written on papyrus, thus explaining the many variations in the four gospels in the New Testament. Moreover, scribes (mostly monks in monasteries) made copies by hand, sometimes adding notes to the margins that may have been inserted into the main text, thus corrupting and mutilating the actual teachings of Jesus. So we can never know exactly what the original writings actually contained because they were edited and translated many times along the way. Neither can we know what may have been added by the Roman Catholic Church for its own purposes throughout the first few centuries. However, the conservative faithful claim it was all divinely inspired by God, if not actually written by him, so its authenticity in any form is not to be challenged. "The Bible says it, I believe it, and that settles it." Moreover, the Bible itself declares its own authenticity: "All scripture is God breathed and profitable" (2 Timothy 3:16) and that "no prophecy of Scripture is a matter of one's own interpretation, for no prophecy was ever made by an act of human will, but men moved by the Holy Spirit spoke from God" (2 Peter 1: 20–21). If true, the Bible is not subject to interpretation, but must be taken as written with faith in its divine authorship, more or less. So let us take it at its own word.

Dr. Loren L. Johns points out that in reading the Bible, especially the historical parts, it is important to keep in mind that at least five levels of development are involved. First, there is the event itself as it may or may not have occurred. Second, there is the understanding of that event that developed over time after the event as God's people passed on the story orally and reflected on its meaning. Third, the event was written down from the perspective of its understood meaning at some later time, sometimes much later, sometimes within a generation. Fourth, at some point years after the writing, the authority of the written story to shape and guide the community of faith was officially recognized and the writing was granted "canonical" (a.k.a. official) status. Fifth, readers who lived in very different cultures and circumstances from ancient times to the present have read these stories and have seen God revealed through them, believe it or not. They seem to be interpreted in a unique way by everyone who reads them. But it is very difficult to determine what scriptures to take merely as interesting history and what to take as mandatory guidelines for living the Christian life today.

Much of the Hebrew Bible or the Old Testament may have been assembled in the fifth century BCE. The Septuagint, sometimes called the Greek Old Testament, is the earliest extant Greek translation of the Old Testament from the original Hebrew. It is estimated that the first five books of the Old Testament, known as the Torah or Pentateuch, were translated in the mid-third-century BCE, and the remaining texts were translated in the second century. The New Testament books were composed largely in the second half of the first century CE. The oldest scraps and pieces of the Old Testament found to date were discovered in caves at Qumran near the northeast corner of the Dead Sea by a young Bedouin shepherd in 1947, known as the "Dead Sea Scrolls." The text of the Dead Sea Scrolls, dated to the first century and before, is written in four different languages: Hebrew, Aramaic, Greek, and Nabataean. The original copies of the Old Testament were written on parchment or papyrus from the time of Moses (c. 1450 BCE) to the time of Malachi (c. 400 BCE). Until the sensational discovery of the Dead Sea Scrolls, we did not possess copies of the Old Testament earlier than 895 CE. The reason for this is that the Jews had an almost superstitious veneration for the text, which impelled them to bury copies that had become too old for use.

After extensive and lengthy analysis by scholars, the conclusion is that the Dead Sea Scrolls have taken biblical scholarship to a new era where much of what was previously believed about the Hebrew text in the Old Testament can now be confirmed, and some of what was accepted as fact should now be reexamined so biblical texts can correspond precisely with what was originally written. In partnership with Google, the Museum of Jerusalem is working to photograph the Dead Sea Scrolls and make them available to the public digitally. Results of this work can be seen by visiting www.deadseascrolls.org.il. A larger collection of ancient manuscripts discovered in 1945 at Nag Hammadi in Egypt deserves mention, but it is dated later and is broader in content than the Dead Sea Scrolls, including some Gnostic texts as well as New Testament contents. Its most discussed item may be the incomplete manuscript of the Gospel of Thomas.

Periodically, scraps of old papyrus manuscripts are found, some dating to the second century. Currently, there are about 136 such pieces in various libraries. The Edict of Milan in 313 CE regarding religious tolerance and marking the end of the persecutions against Christians is seen as the first step toward Christianity becoming the official state religion of the Roman Empire. After many unknown and known manuscripts evolved piecemeal for three centuries by at least fifteen different writers, the first official canon of the complete Bible possibly was compiled by Eusebius, bishop of Caesarea, under orders to provide fifty bibles by Roman emperor Constantine in 331 CE—but no authentic original copies exist. Pope Damasus I is often considered to be the father of the Catholic canon in Latin since what is thought was his list, compiled in 383 CE, corresponds to the current Catholic canon. Origen is the main source of information on the use of the texts that were later officially canonized as the New Testament. The information used to create the late-fourth-century "Easter Letter," which declared accepted Christian writings, was probably based on the lists given in Eusebius's *Ecclesiastical History*, which was primarily based on information provided by Origen. However, in 543 CE, the emperor Justinian I condemned him as a heretic and ordered all his writings to be burned.

Near the end of the fourth century, Christianity was pronounced the official religion of the Roman Empire by its emperor, Theodosius (379–395 CE). Its hierarchical form of government also was the model for organizing the Church. The church of Christ had become the Roman Catholic Church. Dr. Robert M. Price noted, "The Catholic Church is, by ancient design, a closely integrated, massive, and rigidly hierarchical institution. Only so could it ensure uniformity of doctrine, morals, and discipline. Whatever the Church is must come from the top down." By the fifth century, both the Western and Eastern churches had come into agreement on the matter of the New Testament canon. The Catholic canon was reaffirmed at the Council of Trent in 1546, which provided the first "infallible" and effectually promulgated pronouncement on the canon by the Roman Catholic Church. The canons of the Church of England and English Calvinists were decided definitively by the Thirty-Nine Articles (1563) and the Westminster Confession of Faith (1647), respectively. The Synod of Jerusalem (1672) established additional canons that are widely accepted throughout the Eastern Orthodox Church.

The earliest known complete copies of the New Testament are Codex (a.k.a. Book) Sinaiticus and Codex Vaticanus. The latter is cloistered in the Vatican and is largely unavailable for investigation. Both are dated to the early to middle fourth century CE. This means the real story of Jesus is clouded in dark history for about 350 years after his ministry. "Codex" refers to the book form on papyrus used exclusively by early Christians for making copies of biblical writings. Later, they would use parchment scrolls made of animal skins until paper and the printing press were used. Most critical editions of the Greek New Testament and the Old Testament Septuagint give precedence to these two manuscripts, and the majority of translations are based on their text. Nevertheless, there are many differences between these two manuscripts. There are 3,036 textual variations between Sinaiticus and Vaticanus in the text of the four New Testament Gospels alone.

The Codex Sinaiticus is named after the Monastery of Saint Catherine, Mount Sinai, Egypt, where it had been preserved until it was discovered in the oldest Christian library in 1859 by a German scholar named Lobegott Friedrich Constantin (von) Tischendorf under the patronage of Tsar Alexander II of Russia with the active aid of the Russian government. The monastery library preserves the second-largest collection of early codices and manuscripts in the world, outnumbered only by the Vatican Library. It contains Greek, Arabic, Armenian, Coptic, Hebrew, Georgian, Aramaic, and Caucasian Albanian texts. The oldest record of monastic life at Sinai comes from the travel journal written in Latin by a woman named Egeria about 381–384 CE. She visited many places around the Holy Land and Mount Sinai. The monastery was built by order of Roman Emperor Justinian I (527–565 CE), enclosing the Chapel of the Burning Bush ordered to be built by Empress Consort Helena, mother of Constantine the Great, at the site where Moses is supposed to have received the Ten Commandments from God.

Codex Sinaiticus is one of the most important witnesses to the Greek text of the Septuagint, the Old Testament in the version that was adopted by early Greek-speaking Christians, being translated from Hebrew, and the Christian New Testament. No other early manuscript of the Christian Bible has been so extensively analyzed. The handwritten Codex Sinaiticus includes two books that are not part of the official New Testament and at least seven books that are not in the modern Old Testament. The New Testament books are in a different order and include numerous handwritten corrections—some made as much as 800 years after the texts were written. They occurred from those made by the original scribes in the fourth century to ones made in the twelfth century. They range from the alteration of a single letter to the insertion of whole sentences. The principal surviving portion of the Codex, comprising 347 parchment leaves, is now held by the British Library in London, which bought it from Russia in 1933 when Stalin needed the money. A further 43 leaves are kept at the University Library in Leipzig. Parts of 6 leaves are held at the National Library of Russia in Saint Petersburg. Further portions remain at Saint Catherine's Monastery. A small town with hotels and swimming pools called Saint Catherine City has grown around the monastery. The Saint Catherine's Foundation is a UK-based non-profit organization that aims to preserve the monastery.

St. Jerome (347–420 CE) is credited with the first translation of the New Testament into Latin. The New Testament scriptures were controversial even before they were organized into the first authorized canon in the late fourth century. The Roman Catholic Church convened seven ecumenical councils over seven centuries to iron out their differences of interpretation, which still is an ongoing process. Until the modern printing press was invented by Johannes Gutenberg in 1440, the Bible was unavailable to all but Catholic priests, and then only in the Latin version called the Vulgate. The person credited with dividing the Bible into chapters is Stephen Langton, the archbishop of Canterbury from 1207–1228 CE. While Langton's isn't the only organizational scheme that was devised, it is his chapter breakdown that has survived. While chapters are a useful organizational tool, the ability to refer to specific phrases within those chapters would make the system even more usable. French printer Robert Stephanus (a.k.a. Estienne) created a verse numbering system in the midsixteenth century and was the first person to print a Bible with verse numbers in each chapter. There are 1,189 chapters in the King James Bible. The Old Testament contains 929 chapters while the New Testament includes 260 chapters.

Our modern Bible can be traced to the translation by Martin Luther from Latin to German completed in 1534 and then into English with the King James Version in 1611, which many people take as the only "authorized version" since it was authorized by King James I for the Church of England. At this time, Wycliffe Bible translators says the complete Bible has been translated into 670 languages with additional translations of the New Testament into 1,521 different languages of the 6,877 languages known to exist in the world. So a lot of people have not yet gotten its message. Translation has been an issue from the beginning because the meaning and usage of words is not an exact science. Consequently, some of the scriptures literally rendered in English appear to be very confusing. Here is one example from the New International Version:

> *I tell you that anyone who looks at a woman lustfully has already committed adultery with her in his heart (Matthew 5:28) I tell you that anyone who divorces his wife, except for sexual immorality, makes her the victim of adultery, and anyone who marries a divorced woman commits adultery. (Matthew 5:32)*

> *I tell you that anyone who divorces his wife, except for sexual immorality, and marries another woman commits adultery. (Matthew 19:9)*

> *Anyone who divorces his wife and marries another woman commits adultery against her (his wife). And if she divorces her husband and marries another man, she commits adultery. (Mark 10:11–12)*

> *Anyone who divorces his wife and marries another woman commits adultery, and the man who marries a divorced woman commits adultery. (Luke 16:18)*

> *For this reason a man will leave his father and mother and be united to his wife, and the two will become one flesh. So they are no longer two, but one flesh. Therefore, what God has joined together, let no one separate. (Matthew 19:6, Mark 10:8)*

Perhaps we might interpret this instruction with modern information as referring to the merging of egg and sperm to produce a new human being, which, of course, was unknown to the writers.

In addition to linguistic concerns in proof texting, theological issues also drive Bible translations. Some translations of the Bible, produced by single churches or groups of churches, may be influenced by a point of view by the translation committee. For example, the word "love" in most translations is rendered as "charity" in the King James Version (1 Corinthians 13:1–13). Over time, different regions evolved different versions, each with its own assemblage of omissions, additions, and variants.

Many attempts have been made to translate the Bible into modern English, which in this context is defined as the form of English in use after 1800. At this time, there are sixty different English versions available on www.biblegateway.com. In the United States, 55 percent of survey respondents in 2014 who read the Bible reported using the King James Version, followed by 19 percent for the New International Version, with all other versions comprising the rest. The New International Version (NIV), published by Zondervan, is a completely original translation of the Bible developed by more than one hundred scholars from the United States, Canada, the United

Kingdom, Australia, New Zealand, and South Africa, working from the best available Hebrew, Aramaic, and Greek texts. It is revised periodically, the latest in 2011, to assure the most likely translation into modern international usage. I prefer the New International Version, so that is used in this work unless otherwise noted.

The event, the oral tradition and interpretation, the writing, the canonizing, and the reading all take place in different times and circumstances. The assumed presence of God in each of these stages allows modern readers to see a timeless message in the light of their own personal and historical situations. That is the miracle of the Holy Bible.

In the Beginning

To set the stage for the main story of God and his chosen people, the Bible tells of God's good creation and how it got fouled up at the beginning. First, there is the account of the creation of the world from chaos to order—actually, two different versions of it. In the beginning, God created the heavens and the earth. The basic structures of the world—light and darkness, sky and earth, sea and land—were put in place by the word of God; then the general categories of the various inhabitants of that world were added, all in six days. God rested on the seventh day, which set the precedent for observing the Sabbath day. Next, the story focuses specifically on the creation of humans and the fall of humanity into sin through disobedience. The rapid compounding of human evil into violence, all forms of wickedness, and arrogance caused God to take some drastic actions, such as flooding the world (the story of Noah) and scattering the people by confusing their language (the tower of Babel). It seems God preferred that nations should be segregated rather than integrated.

Several of the stories in Genesis 1–11 have parallels in older mythological tales known in Sumeria, an ancient civilization in the Tigris and Euphrates Valley that invented writing around 3000 BCE. For instance, the *Enuma Elish* is an account of a mythological battle among the gods that results in the creation of the world. It is likely that these older tales were known by whoever drew upon these accounts in their writing of the creation accounts in Genesis 1 and 2. Similarly, the story of Noah and the ark likely draws from the well-known *Gilgamesh Epic*, which also features a cataclysmic flood and the salvation of humanity by means of an ark.

Gilgamesh was a legendary priest-king of the Sumerian city-state of Uruk, a major hero in ancient Mesopotamian mythology, and the protagonist of the *Epic of Gilgamesh*, an epic poem written in Akkadian language during the late second millennium BC. He probably ruled sometime between 2800 and 2500 BCE and was posthumously deified. Gilgamesh comes to understand that the most important thing in life is to have lived and loved well.

Our awareness that the biblical stories may be based in part on older mythological tales by no means invalidates the witness of scripture in Genesis 1–11. Rather, it helps us understand the force of the biblical narrative as the writer intended in his time. In contrast to the chaotic and violent *Enuma Elish*, for example, the account of creation in Genesis 1 and 2 emphasizes an orderly, peaceful, and loving God whose creation is purposeful and "good."

The *Enuma Elish* is a Babylonian epic poem written in the Akkadian language and cuneiform script on seven tablets from the late second millennium BCE. It tells the story of how the universe came into being, a great struggle among the gods, and the creation of the world and humanity. The name "Enuma Elish" comes from the first two words of the poem, meaning "when on high" or "when in the heights." The story of *Enuma Elish* has two basic parts. The first involves a cosmogony, that is, the beginning of the universe, and a theogony, that is, the birth of the gods. The second part of the epic tells of the battle between the god Marduk and the chaos dragon Tiamat and how Marduk became the king of the gods and thence creation of humans to serve them.

Central to the stories of Genesis 1–11, which serve to orient the reader to God and to the story of faith that follows, is an emphasis on ethical responsibility. The two original humans, named Adam and Eve, were created in the image of God, male and female, free to choose and fully capable of responding to God. (Does this mean God is both male and female? God is always referred to as He.) He gave them freedom to tend the Garden of Eden but ordered them to avoid eating any fruit from the tree of knowledge of good and evil, lest they surely would die. Having the implied freedom to choose, they nevertheless succumbed to temptation by a serpent to eat of it and thus were alienated from God and cast out of the garden to live like normal human beings lest they should eat of the tree of life and be immortal like the gods. Adam had to work the land for a living, Eve had to suffer in childbirth, and the serpent had to crawl on its belly with enmity between it and humans. Thereafter, flowing through the Bible is the personification of evil, the devil (a.k.a. Satan,) depicted as a "fallen angel" named Lucifer in Isaiah 14:12 (KJV), whose sole purpose seems to be thwarting the will of God. Satan appears fourteen times in the Old Testament and thirty-three times in the New Testament as a real entity to the writers of that time, possibly as the necessary opposite to the Holy Spirit.

The first human offspring were two sons, Cain and Abel. Cain was a farmer, and Abel was a herdsman. Cain killed Abel when he became jealous of him after God preferred his sacrificial burnt offering from his flock while Cain offered the produce from his farm. Cain went unpunished and was protected from harm to become the father of cities—the mother of cities is not explained. Many generations later, the human desire to be independent from or equal to God resulted in the attempt to build a "tower of Babel" that would reach to the heavens. God created multiple languages so they could no longer share information from their natural discoveries in a common tongue. In short, the human refusal to live in submissive relationship to God and to each other resulted in evil of all kinds—jealousy, pride, and murder. Indeed, when he saw how violent and debauched humans had become, God "was sorry that he had made humankind" (Genesis 6:6, 11–12). God actually admitted he made a mistake. So he separated the family of one man, Noah, who was the most righteous, and after instructing him to build a giant floating barge and round up a pair of all landed living creatures, he caused a flood to decimate the earth and thus destroyed all his creation to start over. However, the new humans derived from Noah and his family were no better than the previous ones. The first thing Noah did was plant a vineyard and proceed to get falling down drunk.

The prologue to the Bible story, Genesis 1–11, serves as a religious and moral backdrop to the story that is to follow. It reveals the history of humanity's willful separation from God, a problem to which the rest of the Bible, Genesis 12 through Revelation 22, provides a solution contained in the history and theology of one nomadic tribe and its descendants. Why God chose this one rebellious tribe among all the people on earth, we are not supposed to ask.

After Genesis 12, we see a major shift in the Bible story. The Lord God decided to deal with the problem of this violent and idolatrous piece of humanity that he had created. In this new approach, God started with one family once more to return order and shalom (well-being) to the people and the world he had created. Through the calling and ordering of a people special to God, Christians and Jews claim his will for the whole human race was made known to the world.

Chosen Fathers and Mothers

God's new plan was to call out one family and promise that family and its descendants a future relationship with him as his chosen people. Abraham and Sarah lived about 1800 BCE. At God's call, they left their familiar society in the Euphrates Valley (modern Iraq) to go to a land that the Lord would show them. God's promise was threefold: a land for wandering migrants, children for a barren aged couple, and from that land and with those children God would bring blessings to the following nations (Genesis 12:1–3). He would be their god, and they would be his people. The sign of this special relationship would be the circumcision of all male children on their eighth day. God promised Abraham he would have a son to begin the chain of heirs to extend the promise into many nations. Such promises were hard to fulfill, as the aging Abraham and Sarah, their son Isaac and Rebekah, and their grandson, Jacob and Rachel, their descendants, found out.

Because he was doubtful and impatient, Abraham fathered a son named Ishmael with Hagar, the servant of Sarah, at her suggestion. When their promised son was born later, they rejected Ishmael and his mother and cast them into the desert where God took care of them and promised them a great inheritance also. Abraham gained the favor of God by demonstrating he was willing to offer his only son, Isaac, as a blood sacrifice. Isaac fathered twins, Jacob and Esau. Fulfilling the prophecy of God and obeying the intrigue of his mother, Jacob stole the inheritance from Esau, the firstborn son, by impersonating him to their nearly blind father, Isaac. Thus, the legal inheritance of Esau was thwarted by fraud. Jacob fathered twelve sons, the youngest of whom, Joseph, was to become the protector and savior of the family and its descendants from starvation. The promised land of Canaan at the eastern end of the Mediterranean Sea lay between the great political powers in Mesopotamia and in Egypt. Suffering plagued the family in each generation, as well as mounting sibling jealousies and quarrels. Time and again, problems would arise, and it began to look as if God's promises would never be fulfilled. In addition, occasional famines caused devastation and finally made it necessary for the chosen family, by then amounting to seventy souls, to leave the land and journey into Egypt to survive.

Only after Abraham's great-grandson Joseph, the youngest of twelve brothers from the house of Jacob (thence called Israel), who, through great suffering after he was sold off into slavery by his jealous siblings, rose to a position next to the king/pharaoh of Egypt, did any significant blessing come to the Hebrew tribes. After his faithful loyalty provided an opening for him to serve the ruling pharaoh, the lust and dishonest accusation by his wife landed Joseph in prison. However, by using his talent in dream interpretation, Joseph was called to manage the country through seven years of famine and reunited his family of seventy relatives to enjoy a time of comfort in the land of Goshen. Unfortunately, this favor was changed into tragedy and suffering after succeeding kings of Egypt bound the Hebrews into slavery as the authority of Joseph faded into history.

At the end of the book of Genesis, and some 400 years later, the promise was still alive because of their tenacious faith. But the only land they possessed in Canaan was a burial plot, and the family descendants were still in Egypt, outside the promised land, and enslaved by new rulers who had forgotten the saga of Joseph. However, despite setback after setback, God would eventually keep his promise to the ancestors of Abraham and return them to the promised land.

Slavery, Exodus, and Covenant

The story picks up in Exodus, second book of the Bible, with God's people in Egypt—not as the favored kinfolk of Joseph, but as slaves of pharaoh (the title for the king). They were conscripted into building cities and monuments for him. From remnants visible today, the buildings were sights to behold—such as the temple at Karnak. The Egyptians treated them as a slave people and made their lives miserable (Exodus 1:14). But God saw their misery and heard their cries, and after 400 years, he acted! It seems more than a little odd that the god who saved the tribes of Israel from a disastrous famine would disappear while their heirs were enslaved in the same place they were saved. God works in mysterious ways.

Again, God called a servant. This time, God the "I AM" called a deliverer, Moses, (1350–1250 BCE). He was raised in the court of pharaoh after being discovered abandoned by his Hebrew mother to escape the genocide that was ordered to reduce the population of Jews. Moses was familiar both with the royal court of the king, being raised as a prince although a Hebrew, and also with life in the desert. He was married and living in exile to escape arrest for killing a slave master in a fit of rage. Moses left his family and returned to Egypt to set his people free after accepting the assignment reluctantly when God called him out of a burning bush. (God seems to like talking through burning bushes.) The terrible struggle for their freedom is told in stories of two miracles and ten plagues, which were necessary to overcome the refusal of pharaoh to let the people go, as was his destiny, which God admitted causing by hardening Pharaoh's heart, so he could send the plagues (Exodus 4:21, 10:20, 27, 11:10, 14:4). Did you get that?

Although he intentionally hardened the heart of Pharaoh, God used natural elements invoked by Moses, such as blood in the Nile River, bugs, and dust storms, frogs, and locusts to overcome Pharaoh's stubbornness, which God caused and set the people free. The plagues culminated in the death of Egypt's firstborn children, including his own son, while those of the Hebrews were spared as the angel of death "passed over" their homes. Pharaoh finally relented and let the Israelites go, only to change his mind and pursue them to the sea thence to be totally vanquished with rushing waves that devoured his entire army, horses, carriages, and all. Once again, God used the elements of nature—wind and sea—to save the Hebrew people and thwart their enemy. "Yahweh," the name of God revealed to Moses, is depicted as a warrior-deliverer; and the descendants of Abraham, Isaac, and Jacob were free at last!

But free for what? Free to face the deadly desert, free to face an uncertain future because they were accustomed to being governed by others. For both situations, they needed a guiding and providing presence. Facing hunger and thirst in the desert, they complained bitterly, but the Lord sent food supplies from heaven, and Moses found water by striking a rock. Facing an unstructured future, they received from God laws and rules pronounced by Moses to ensure just social structures.

There in the Sinai desert, Yahweh-God entered into a covenant to be their God if the Hebrew people, now numbering several hundred thousand, would obey his instruction and forsake all other gods, of which there were many. Moses, their deliverer, was now the covenant mediator and lawgiver. The Ten Commandments, delivered by God to Moses on Mount Sinai, formed the basic stipulations of the covenant. The law codes written up by Moses spelled out in great detail how the people were to live in holy faithfulness. All together, there were 613 do's and don'ts to live by. Moses declared, "If you pay attention to these laws and are careful to follow them, then the Lord your God will keep his covenant of love with you, as he swore to your ancestors" (Deuteronomy 7:12).

God had heard the people's cries of suffering and delivered them from slavery and brought them out of Egypt into a special relationship with him. God had acted and had shown the people his grace. Now the people were called upon to respond submissively and obediently to that grace by doing what was commanded toward God in keeping the covenant agreement. Yahweh's double-sided grace of deliverance and covenant law, when combined with the people's obedience, formed them into God's priestly kingdom, whose purpose it was to bring God's will to life—giving prosperity to all the nations to follow (Exodus 19:4–6).

Settlement in the Promised Land

The chosen people were afraid and wanted to return to Egypt, and some rebelled against Moses and against God. When they were tempted by the Midianites to worship other gods, Moses ordered his warrior captains to kill all the males and married women, leaving only the young virgins for themselves (Numbers 31:13–18). When the elders rebelled at invading the promised land for fear of their lives, Moses delayed their attack until the elder generation died off—some forty years—because they were not worthy to inherit the land yet. So it would be their children who would possess the promised Canaan land. Moses, the deliverer and covenant maker, was not allowed to enter the promised land before he died, reminding the Israelites of the consequences if they should abandon the covenant made with the Lord.

Leadership passed to his aide, Joshua, sometime around 1220 BCE. How the promised land of Canaan came to be occupied is uncertain because the biblical accounts disagree somewhat. The account in the book of Joshua—the longer, simpler, and popular account—tells of a blitzkrieg-type invasion and genocide by the united tribes of Israel under Joshua, as ordered by God, which wiped out the six tribes of Canaanites and allowed the settlement of the land. The account in Judges implies that the Hebrews slowly infiltrated the land, taking control of the tribal areas, while continuing to suffer from the presence of troublesome pockets of Canaanite peoples who naturally resisted their invasion and occupation. Archaeological evidence suggests yet a third scenario: that individual clans joined forces with disenfranchised peasants within Canaan and rose up and took control of the land from the wealthy landowners from an internal revolution. It seems most likely that some combination of the above three possibilities accounted for Israel's settlement of Canaan. In Canaan, Judah (descendants of the first son of Jacob) became the main tribe in the south while Ephraim (a Joseph tribe) became the main tribe in the north.

With no central governing authority, but with a central shrine (the tabernacle housing the Ten Commandments in a golden-trimmed ark) brought along from the desert, the people were ruled by a series of tribal "judges." The book of Judges mentions twelve leaders who judged Israel: Othniel, Ehud, Shamgar, Deborah, Gideon, Tola, Jair, Jephthah, Ibzan, Elon, Abdon, and Samson. The First Book of Samuel mentions Eli and Samuel, as well as Joel and Abiah (two sons of Samuel). The First Book of Chronicles mentions Kenaniah and his sons. The Second Book of Chronicles mentions Amariah and Zebadiah). If they ruled consecutively, some scholars estimate the period of judges lasted about 400 years. Life was hard, and the neighboring peoples threatened their lives, so the chosen people were in constant battles, both defensive and offensive.

Because there was no strong central authority in the form of a king, "everyone did what was right in his [or her] own eyes." When the people obeyed the covenant stipulations through the edicts of Moses, things went well, but when they disobeyed, they began to be oppressed. In response to the cries of the people, the Lord would send a leader, and God's people would be saved. Comfortable once again, God's people would soon disobey, and God would again cause his people to be oppressed by a foreign enemy. When they repented and called out to God, he would again send a deliverer (a "judge"), and so the cycle continued.

God's active leadership through Joshua and the judges is offset by the wavering faith of the people, who often abandoned God and the laws of Moses. It was a difficult and violent time, and the cry went up for stronger human leadership, for a king.

The Kings and Prophets

Sometime about 1050 BCE, the last great judge, Samuel, appeared on the stage. He combined in his life the roles of judge, priest, and prophet. As the transition figure between the tribal period and the time of the kingdom, he was the one to anoint the first kings: Saul and then David.

There was divided opinion about the need for a king. One group, which apparently included Samuel, believed that a king would interfere with Yahweh's direct rule over the people. But the other group, anxious about the continued threat of the Philistines, wanted the security of central rule, with a military deliverer and strong leadership like their neighbors had (1 Samuel 9–10). The latter group prevailed, but Samuel laid down the limits of kingship, that is, "the rights and duties" of kings (1 Samuel 10:25) and warned about potential abuses of a monarchy. He was to be proven deadly right.

Kings

Saul, the first king of Israel, was much like the previous judges in that his kingship was driven by direct orders from God. A man of considerable stature and military leadership, he eventually succumbed to jealousy and depression over the success and popularity of his ward, young David from the house of Jesse—chosen by Samuel and called to defeat the giant Philistine, Goliath, in battle. David was raised in the court of Saul and became a thorn in his side as the young man developed in favor with the Lord and friendship with Jonathan, son of the king. Through a series of precipitous and ill-advised decisions to wage war, when he disobeyed instructions to complete genocide against his enemies, Saul lost the favor of God and was killed in battle along with his son, Jonathan, the rising king.

David became the first great king of Israel around 1000 BCE by establishing the kingdom of Israel on the level of the great kingdoms of the world. At first, he was the king of Judah in the south. Later, he was anointed king of all Israel including the northern kingdom. One of his stellar acts was to capture Jerusalem from the Jebusites and to make it his capital, his own personal city, and the religious center of Israel, that is, the city of David.

David was a man of faith, a poet, a musician (the reason many psalms are attributed to him), a conquering military strategist, and a great administrator. He was also popular with the people; he won their hearts by winning many battles. The people sang out, "Saul has killed thousands but David has killed ten thousands." To this great king was given the third great promise of the Bible, the promise of an everlasting dynasty in which his sons as kings would be "sons of God" (2 Samuel 7).

But David had a weakness: the arrogance of great success. This led him to commit adultery, murder, and a long series of troubles within his own family. Although King David was brilliant and successful, he also suffered a lot and thus came to be the model for a messiah. He was enabled to conquer and occupy Jerusalem, hence called the "City of David." And although David was popular with the people, later biblical tradition suggests that God did not allow him to build a temple to Yahweh in Jerusalem because he was violent, and he had shed so much blood as a warrior (1 Chronicles 22:8, 28:3). His adultery with Bathsheba and de facto murder of her husband in battle caused the death of their firstborn son as punishment, so the crown was to be passed to the second heir.

King Solomon succeeded his father David and tried to outdo him in worldly power and splendor. Among his many building projects, he erected the temple in Jerusalem, which became the center of the official national religion with its priesthood and ceremonies. In addition to his building endeavors, Solomon is noted for his riches and his wisdom, plus his wives and concubines. The book of Proverbs, the book of Ecclesiastes, the Song of Songs, and other wisdom writings are attributed to him. On the other hand, his many wives and concubines were his undoing since they led him into the worship of false gods that they brought with them from conquered lands.

Among the more significant accomplishments of Solomon was the growth of Israel's government structures. To finance the building of the temple and his other impressive building projects, Solomon taxed the people heavily. While the improved infrastructure provided new means for growth and prosperity, such as new and expanded international trade opportunities, the common person found the heavy taxation burdensome. When his son, Rehoboam, made it clear that he intended to continue and expand Solomon's policy of heavy taxation and big government, the people revolted.

After the death of Solomon, the kingdom of Israel split into two: Judah in the south and Israel in the north. Regional cultural differences existed between the south and the north, and there was great resentment, especially in the north, of Rehoboam's forced labor policies.

The northern kingdom of Israel was larger and more prosperous, but also more unstable. It experienced several changes of dynasty in its two-hundred-year history (922–722 BCE). The best-known king was also the most infamous, Ahab and his queen Jezebel, because they officially supported the worship of foreign fertility gods. The powerful Assyrians, longtime enemies of Israel with their capital at Nineveh, eventually destroyed Samaria, the capital of Israel, and took the leading citizens away as exiles. Thus, in 722 BCE, this part of the history of the people of God came to a tragic end.

However, the southern kingdom of Judah continued for another 135 years. The dynasty of David survived those years, even with many evil kings who engaged in almost continuous warfare against the adjacent kingdoms. There are so many battles recorded in the books of Kings there must be many thousands of shallow graves under the sands of the Middle East. Wars at that time were fought with swords, spears, and bows, and there was no battlefield medical care for the wounded. The recruitment, arming, training, support, and maintenance of such large armies can only be imagined, even by modern standards. Only two kings of Israel received high marks from the "Deuteronomistic historian," the assumed historian responsible for the final editing of Joshua, Judges, Samuel, and Kings in the sixth century BCE. Hezekiah at the end of the 700s BCE and Josiah about seventy-five years later were the two kings noted for their faithfulness and reforms.

Despite repeated warnings through the prophets, especially Isaiah and Jeremiah, the people of Judah had managed to convince themselves that God was on their side and they were invincible; no foreign country could ever seriously threaten them. Had not God promised that Zion (i.e., Jerusalem) would be their dwelling place forever (Exodus 32:13; 2 Kings 21:7)? Had not God promised that a descendant of David would sit on the throne in Jerusalem forever (2 Samuel 7:13–16; 1 Kings 9:5)? These promises had lulled the people into a spiritual complacency, a complacency that was soon to result in their downfall.

In 586 BCE, the city of Jerusalem, along with the temple, was destroyed by the invading Babylonians, who carried away its leading citizens to exile in Babylon. However, it was through this Diaspora group that the story of the Jewish people continued through the people of Judah in exile, who are now beginning to call themselves Jews.

Leaders of God's People

The king was the Lord's CEO, chief executive officer, responsible for the well-being of the people. It was his job to see that the affairs of the nation, both domestic and foreign, were conducted justly and in loyalty to Yahweh under the Sinai covenant.

The priests from the tribe of Levi were responsible for the regular or ordinary will of God by conducting the ceremonies and teaching the Torah (law or covenant stipulations). By regular will of God, we mean the will of God revealed in the law codes and traditions of the people.

The prophets were the watchers who checked the spiritual health of the nation. They noted when and how the king and/or people departed from the path of righteousness (keeping things right according to the revealed will of God) and boldly declared what God's will meant in terms of national welfare. We might say that the prophets looked after the extraordinary, that is, the circumstantial will of the Lord.

The sages were those senior persons in the community who served as teachers of the leaders. These maintainers of the wisdom tradition were the especially astute observers of human nature and circumstances. They passed on wisdom in the practical affairs of life not specifically covered in the rules of the Torah. As in any society, when all these persons did their jobs, life was good, there was shalom, the people "lived long in the land," and the Lord could say, "I will be your God, and you shall be my people" (Jeremiah 7:23).

What went wrong? The people of Israel were intended to be the kingdom of God. The king was the "son of God" (not a supernatural being), the one who was to be God's servant-ruler. The temple in the city of Jerusalem was to be the place where the Lord was to be worshipped by a proper priesthood in proper ceremonies. The people under the rule of God's king and the guidance of God's prophets were to be the covenant people obedient to and prospered by God.

But it was not to be. Kings and the chosen people did not keep the covenant, and it appeared that the promises of God could not be kept after 586 BCE. The leading citizens were out of the promised land in exile. There was no longer a Davidic king. The temple had been destroyed, and the priesthood was not functioning. This supreme crisis had scattered the people and shattered the faith. It was not clear whether there would be a continuing people of Yahweh-God.

Exile and After

Israel, the northern kingdom, was taken into exile to Nineveh and passed out of Bible history in 722 BCE. Was the same thing to happen to the southern kingdom, Judah, in 586 BCE when they were taken into exile in Babylon? It looked like it might be the end of God's great experiment; all the promises seemed to be broken, and the people were demoralized. The history books from Deuteronomy to Kings told why the disaster happened: the people had willfully and continually disobeyed the covenant God had made with the chosen people at Mount Sinai. The prophets before the exile had said the same thing in dramatic and urgent terms. Jeremiah declared that there would be seventy years of exile (Jeremiah 29:10).

Actually, the condition of the Hebrew exiles in Babylon was not that difficult. They were not prisoners of war but forcibly resettled immigrants who could establish their own businesses and cultivate their own farms. Economically and perhaps politically, the peasants who were left in Israel and Judah were worse off. What the exiles in Babylon suffered was the sense of being separated from the sacred land and the sacred Temple, with its priesthood, rituals, and ceremonies. In this crisis-of-faith situation, a serious rethinking of the covenant took place. The prophet Ezekiel was a dominant figure in that rethinking, as was the author of Isaiah 40–55.

About forty-five years after Jerusalem was destroyed and the people were transported to Babylon, a new political star was rising in the east, and a new empire was forming. Cyrus, king of the Persian Empire, permitted all exiled peoples (not only Jews) to return to their native lands. His decree recorded in Ezra 1 and on Cyrus's Cylinder signaled the "new exodus" foretold by the prophet (Jeremiah 31:2–14, 28). But only a minority of the Jewish exiles returned; the others were well established in their new environment, and the sacred place was not that important to them.

Those who did return found a society in shambles. Judah was now a small province of the Persian Empire that was physically broken down and populated with a demoralized people. As Jeremiah had said, the Lord was going to "pluck and break down" before turning to "build and plant." According to the account, one of the first things to be rebuilt was the temple. Over about twenty years, with great opposition from enemy neighbors, but with the encouragement of the prophets Haggai and Zechariah, the modest second temple was completed. In the succeeding decades, things did not go well. Apparently, the law either was not observed at all or was observed only halfheartedly. Economic and political structures were weak and disorganized.

About eighty years after the return of the Diaspora from exile, Ezra, the priest and scribe, brought a new edition of the law and energetically worked to promulgate and enforce it. If the reason for the earlier judgment by the Lord was not keeping the law, then the obvious remedy was to keep it more carefully. This was Ezra's mission. But other problems remained. Nehemiah, a rising Jewish official in the Persian court, asked permission to return to Judah and serve as governor. The endeavor for which he is remembered is the rebuilding of the city wall. This task represented the reestablishment of economic order and a limited degree of political and military self-sufficiency.

Thus, at the end of the Old Testament, things seem to be recovering slowly. But the complaint still was, "We are slaves" within the Persian Empire (Nehemiah 9:36).

The cycle of history outlined in Judges chapter 2 had come full circle. The period starting with the deliverance from Egypt and the covenant at Sinai under Moses, followed by the genocide and occupation of the promised land of Canaan under Joshua, was seen as one of general faithfulness. The following time of the kingdom, beginning with Saul and David, though it had its ups and downs, was viewed by the prophets as a time of disobedience and unfaithfulness. Punishment in the form of double defeat and exile came next, followed by the promised new exodus, renewal, and reform.

Thus, Old Testament history ends on a mildly optimistic note. But the prophetic literature held even greater promises concerning an ideal king and a glorious age to come. The great promises of God to Abraham, Moses, and David had not been neglected, only delayed. Their fulfillment had been postponed, and hope was often abandoned. Nevertheless, those promises of God still stood, and they would be fulfilled, though perhaps in unexpected forms.

Other Writings in the Old Testament

We have been following the general outline of the books of Moses (the Pentateuch or Torah), the history books, and the prophets. These books carry the story of the Bible through the covenant with Abraham and the lives of the Jews. But another group of books has a different purpose. This group is called the "Writings." The Pentateuch, or first five books of the Old Testament, is often called the "Law." The historical books of Joshua, Judges, Samuel, and Kings are often called the "Former Prophets," and the writing prophets the "Latter Prophets." The third major category in the Bible, the "Writings," actually is a miscellaneous category consisting of late writings—whether historical, such as Chronicles; or prophetic, such as Daniel; Psalms; and wisdom literature.

The book of Psalms is the hymnbook of the Bible, the "praises of Israel," humanity's response to the nature and activities of God. While praise or trust is the dominant attitude, lament is the most common type of psalm. This book is probably the most used part of the Bible. It reflects the piety of Israel in all its gritty boldness, expressing praise and lament, anger and frustration, hope and despair, doubt and thanksgiving—all directed by Israel toward Yahweh, their God.

The book of Proverbs is a collection of wisdom sayings growing out of the observation of what constitutes the "good life." Many things in life do not fall under legal limits; they are not subject to laws. Such things are deemed wise or foolish; they lead to good or bad consequences. The book of Proverbs is a word to the wise and those who wish to be wise.

Ecclesiastes and Job are deep probes of the traditional moral view of life in a world full of suffering. They represent a more skeptical form of wisdom literature, even challenging conventional wisdom at times. What is the worth, they ask, of much that we value, such as hard work, if it all comes to nothing in death? After all, when you're dead, you're dead. Why is it that sometimes the righteous suffer for no apparent reason? Is there any real value in this life to serving God? One may acquire vast wealth and power in the world and still feel bereft. With much wisdom comes much grief, and with much knowledge comes much sorrow. (Ecclesiastes 1:18) We may suffer and lose everything, but God is the ruler yet. Job declares the Lord gives and the Lord takes away—may the Lord be praised. (Job 1:21)

The Song of Songs (or the Songs of Solomon) is a collection of love poetry designed to show the beauty of human love and romance or, as some say, an allegory of passionate love for God. The book of Ruth recalls that the great-grandmother of King David had been a foreigner, a Moabitess. It represents a challenge to those quarters of Judaism that linked Jewish identity with ethnic purity.

Another great woman of the faith was Esther, who was elevated to the high position of queen of Persia. Basic to all this "wisdom literature" is the attempt to understand God's actions in the world in ways that can make sense to people seeking the truth about God and human experience.

Between the Testaments: 400 BCE to Jesus

A four-hundred-year gap exists between the last events recorded in the Old Testament and the time of Jesus in the New Testament. The only canonical exception to this silent period is the book of Daniel, written around 170 BCE in the midst of one of the biggest challenges to the faith of Israel in the intertestamental period. Fortunately, the Apocrypha, especially the book of 1 Maccabees, the Old Testament Pseudepigrapha (some fifty texts of falsely attributed works), Jewish writings from this period of time that were never canonized, and the Dead Sea Scrolls, which date from the second century BCE to the first century CE, provide helpful windows on this time period.

Three main events dominated this period, and their repercussions were extensive. Alexander the Great conquered the huge territory ranging from Greece in the west to Pakistan in the east, including Palestine and Egypt, around 333 BCE. Along with his military conquests came the spread of Greek language and culture. This spreading influence, known as Hellenism, is not unlike the spread of American culture around the world today.

Along with the spread of Greek language and culture came the spread of Greek religion. But how should the faithful Jew respond to this new culture, language, and religion? Should it be resisted? Should it be embraced, the answer of the "Letter to Aristeas" in the Old Testament Pseudepigrapha? Should part of it be embraced and part of it resisted?

Conservative Jews resented pagan Hellenism and agreed that its spread must be resisted. But how? Should they take up arms, the answer of 1 Enoch and 1 Maccabees, or should they resist nonviolently, the answer of Daniel?

When Seleucid Antiochus IV, "Epiphanes"—a self-imposed nickname meaning "God manifest"—took the throne of Syria and Palestine in 175 BCE, he decided to be more intentional and consistent about the Hellenization of his subjects than ever before. He made it illegal to offer sacrifices to Yahweh in the temple or to circumcise a baby. In short, he outlawed Judaism. He went so far as to desecrate the temple in Jerusalem by marching into the Holy of Holies—where only the high priest was to enter, and then only once a year on the Day of Atonement—and he proceeded to sacrifice a pig, which is ritually unclean to the Jews, on the altar to his god, Baal Shemesh, or Zeus.

As a result, the Jews revolted. This Maccabean revolt was the second important event. After about twenty-five years of fighting, the Jews gained independence from what was left of the Greek empire. Their independence under a group of Jewish rulers called the Hasmoneans lasted from 142 to 63 BCE. That eighty-year period was the first since 586 BCE—and the last until 1948 CE—that Jewish leaders had control over their own land.

Although this revolt began with high motives to provide a kingdom in which Yahweh could be worshipped properly without interference from foreign influence, the Hasmonean dynasty soon deteriorated into a typical Hellenistic tyranny, complete with its own paranoid and cutthroat power politics, including the murder by Jews of fellow Jews who criticized Hasmonean policies. When a dispute arose in the sixties about who would be the next legitimate Hasmonean king, the Romans stepped in to restore orderly government. However, that rescue in 63 BCE came at a high cost: the Jewish people were again put under foreign domination.

In the meantime, the form of religious faith called Judaism, which had roots going back to Ezra, continued to grow and develop. The twin emphases of keeping the law and observing the temple rituals, with its calendar of festivals, characterized this movement of Jewish religion as different from Israel's earlier faith. Accompanying and spurring these emphases was the rise of the synagogue as a local place of worship and instruction in the law.

In the second century BCE, several Jewish religious parties developed around differing visions about how God's people should understand and maintain their identity. Immediately below the surface of the identity question was the issue of how and how much faithful Jews should resist Hellenism.

The resulting parties consisted of the *Pharisees*, the *Sadducees*, the *Essenes*, and the *Zealots*. The *Sadducees* were a priestly aristocratic group that ran the temple establishment, held public offices, and cooperated with the Roman overlords. They were the conservative establishment group who advocated compromise and acceptance of Hellenism as long as their system of temple worship was not threatened. This group had perhaps the most to gain from cooperating with the Romans: not only continued control of the temple, but also the high standard of living deriving from their temple activities. For the *Sadducees*, the Torah alone—the first five books—were authoritative. The prophets were perhaps interesting, but not ultimately useful for determining doctrine.

The *Pharisees* were a nonpriestly or lay group that took the keeping of the law, in both written and oral forms, very seriously. The oral law allowed them to adapt the written law to changing circumstances, and by the time of Jesus, the law was a hodge-podge of rules and regulations scarcely followed by anyone. They advocated a clear and courageous resistance to Hellenism, but not organized, violent resistance. The *Pharisees* were optimistic about the possibility of complete faithfulness to God, if one were fully committed to it. They also tended to look down on the common person who could not afford all the sacrifices required for full compliance to the law of Moses.

The *Essenes* were convinced that everyone else was lax, if not evil. The Essenes were a priestly group whose origins stemmed from the second century BCE when a new line of priests took control of the temple. The *Essenes* believed that of all the Jews, only they were acceptable to God. As a result, they withdrew into separated communities, such as the community at Qumran near the Dead Sea.

They were very rigid in observing the law, especially laws concerning purity and the religious calendar, and looked forward to the Day of the Lord in which they would serve as soldiers in God's final war. One of the Dead Sea Scrolls even contains detailed instructions for how to fight in this Final Battle.

The *Zealots* represented a fourth option. It is questionable whether a continuous organized movement of Zealots existed from 167 BCE to 66 CE, when the *Zealots* led the first Jewish revolt against Rome; "Zealotism" was illegal, and its adherents were forced underground. Nevertheless, "Zealotism" remained a clear and present theoretical option to Jews, and throughout this period, several Zealot leaders and movements arose. These *Zealots* advocated bold and violent resistance to the evils of pagan Hellenism, even if it meant death, for in their view, their own resistance was a continuation of the Maccabean concern to "throw out the pagan foreigners."

Prominent in the diverse forms of Judaism at the turn of the millennia was *apocalyptic* thought. Sometimes apocalypticism took a revolutionary form, but it usually counseled waiting for the Lord to intervene in a cataclysmic way to defeat all evil forces and to set the world aright. Faithful Jews who held this viewpoint developed a literature using dramatic symbols and visions.

Another school of thought was indebted to the wisdom tradition and developed a literature much like the wisdom literature of the Old Testament. The book of Daniel, which probably comes from this period, includes both of these viewpoints, wisdom and apocalyptic. The Apocrypha and other writings not included in the Jewish or Christian canons (the Old Testament Pseudepigrapha) were products of this era. The Apocrypha, included in the Catholic Bible, contains history and wisdom literature while the Old Testament Pseudepigrapha also contains apocalyptic writings, but from unknown authors.

Jesus and the Kingdom of God: BCE–30 CE

The stage was finally set for the coming of God's special son, which launched the New Testament. The Roman occupation and the Jewish hierarchy were in control of politics and religious activities in the province of Judea. Both levied taxes under which the people suffered. The various Jewish religious groups formed a spectrum of resistance ideologies, from willing cooperation with the Romans to opposition by violence. All groups emphasized the keeping of the law and of the temple rituals, though in different degrees.

The Pharisees were the most influential group, but it is estimated that membership in all four of the groups or "philosophies" constituted only 10 percent of the population. The other 90 percent were the ordinary people of the land who had neither the interest nor the leisure to pursue religious or political activities beyond the minimum. Everyone, of course, hoped for deliverance from their bondage by God in one form or another.

Non-Christian writings in the first century (Greek, Roman/Latin, and Hebrew) yield only the barest mentions concerning Jesus, so there is practically no secular corroboration of the Bible narrative. The extensive Roman history of the times, written by Pliny the Elder (23–79 CE), contains no mention of Jesus. Only Jewish historian Flavius Josephus gives an account of him in his *Antiquities of the Jews* (93–94 CE):

> About this time there lived Jesus, a wise man, if indeed one ought to call him a man. For he was one who performed surprising deeds and was a

teacher of such people as accept the truth gladly. He won over many Jews and many of the Greeks. He was (believed to be) the Christ. And when, upon the accusation of the principal men among us, Pilate had condemned him to a cross, those who had first come to love him did not cease. He appeared to them spending a third day restored to life, for the prophets of God had foretold these things and a thousand other marvels about him. And the tribe of the Christians, so called after him, has still to this day not disappeared.

Some scholars wonder if this passage is authentic and may have been inserted by Jewish Christian scribes. Writing no later than 324 CE, Bishop of Rome Eusebius quotes the passage in essentially the same form as that preserved in extant manuscripts. So part or all of the passage in Pliny may have been inserted by Eusebius or others to provide an outside Jewish authority for the life of Christ.

Origen (184–253 CE), "the greatest genius the early church produced," wrote that Josephus did not recognize Jesus as the Christ when mentioning him in the *Antiquities of the Jews*. Josephus is the only secular source to mention John the Baptist and his execution by Herod. Because manuscript copying was done by hand, typically by monastic scribes, almost all ancient texts have been subject to both accidental and deliberate alterations. Although there is no doubt that most of the later copies of the *Antiquities* contained references to Jesus and John the Baptist, it cannot be proved that these were in the original Josephus writings. Some scholars claim they are purely fabrications, some claim they are authentic, and some offer a compromise, so the matter remains unsettled. Wikipedia cites 153 sources in its discussion of Josephus.

Thus, the four Gospels of the New Testament are the only extensive source for the life of Jesus, although his teachings and key events in his life are referenced in the Acts of the Apostles and the letters by Paul. Though the Gospel of Thomas found in the Dead Sea Scrolls has recently been touted as a major new original source for the historical Jesus, it likely dates from the second century CE, and its traditions are heavily overlaid with the influence of the Gnostic heresy.

The books titled Matthew, Mark, and Luke have a similar outline and outlook and are therefore called Synoptic Gospels. (The word *synoptic* means "similar point of view.") Scholars think Mark is the oldest manuscript dating a decade or so after the crucifixion. Matthew and Luke present more details presumably because the oral tradition was embellished as time passed. The Gospel of John is quite different in outline, incidents reported, and the manner in which Jesus's life is presented because it may be infused with Gnostic beliefs, according to some scholars.

Although his parents lived in Nazareth, scripture says they had to go to Bethlehem for a census where Jesus was born in a stable, apparently without a midwife, about 6 BCE probably in the spring because the calendar is a bit off. Our Gregorian calendar is named after Pope Gregory XIII, who introduced it in October 1582. The last country to adopt it was Greece in 1923. The Gospel of Matthew tells us that Herod the Great was the king in Israel, and it is known that Herod died in 4 BCE. The birth of Jesus was attended by some wise men or shepherds or both (Matthew 2:1–2, Luke 2:8–9). Celebration of his birth on December 25 was not firmly established until the late third century, but its origin remains unknown. Isaac Newton suggested it may have been associated with a festival of lights to mark the winter solstice when the sun begins its return after the annual precession of the earth completes its cycle. The first recorded Christmas celebration was in Rome in 336 CE.

Specific mention of the term "Christmas" or its religious aspects is being increasingly censored, avoided, or discouraged by a number of advertisers, retailers, government, and other public and private organization. The public holiday has become a major economic event in many countries as the exchange of presents creates a major retail sales opportunity.

Whether his mother, Mary, and his father, Joseph, were divinely chosen has been debated endlessly. Scripture says Mary was a virgin, but some scholars say this may be a mistranslation and could be "young woman." In 1854, Pope Pius IX declared her immaculate conception, that is, born without sin. But the scriptures specifically state that her conception of Jesus was an act of the Holy Spirit, which is never really defined in scriptures (Matthew 1:23, Luke 1:29–30). Scripture says he was named Jesus on the day he was circumcised in obedience to the instructions of the angel who foretold his birth to Mary (Luke 2:21). But this conflicts with other scriptures that say he was to be named Immanuel, meaning "God is with us" (Isaiah 7:17, Matthew 1:23). Astrologers told Herod, the king of Israel, the newborn was prophesied to be a king of the Jews, so he ordered all newborn boys less than two years old to be slain in a vain attempt to destroy Jesus. But Joseph and Mary were forewarned and fled with the child to exile in Egypt (Matthew 2).

After a period of refuge in Egypt to escape the murder of infants ordered by Herod until after he died, the family returned to Nazareth (which is present today), where Jesus grew to adulthood in an observant Jewish family of five brothers—James, Joseph, Simon, and Judas/Jude—and unnamed sisters, apparently engaged in the occupation of carpentry. Indeed, Jesus could do no faith-based miracles in his hometown of Nazareth because the neighbors all recalled him as "the carpenter's son" (Matthew 13:55). Jesus probably died at Passover weekend in the spring of 30 CE. Nothing is known of his youth, except he was found in discourse with scribes in the temple at his age of twelve. He could discuss weighty matters with the "doctors of the law," the scribes and priests who spent a lifetime studying the written law and the oral commentary. After this account, Jesus disappears until about his age of thirty. The Bible merely states, "And Jesus grew in wisdom and stature, and in favor with God and man" (Luke 2:52). This really is a curious omission for one claimed to be the Messiah.

John the Baptist, described in Luke as a cousin of Jesus, roamed the wilderness in animal skins while eating locusts and honey, proclaiming, "Repent and be baptized because the Kingdom of Heaven is at hand." When Jesus was baptized by John about his age of thirty, a voice from heaven identified him as God's son (i.e., God's anointed king [Psalm 2] and as the servant of God who would suffer for the sake of his people [Isaiah 42:1–9; 52:13–53:12]). He went about announcing the approach of the "Kingdom of God" or the "Kingdom of heaven"; that is, God's domain over life (Mark 1:14–15). He claimed that he came from heaven, the domain of his Father, that he spoke as his Father directed him to, and that his death and resurrection were necessary to atone for the sins of many, that he would return to heaven and come back again at some future time to set up a kingdom on earth after all evil is vanquished. Those who believed in him would inherit eternal life, and those who did not would be cast into hell (Luke 12:5).

Jesus directed his sharpest judgment, while claiming to be non-judgmental, against hypocrites, those who do not practice what they preach but, in fact, do the opposite. He condemned hypocrites fifteen times in the Gospels. He judged the Pharisees thus:

> You brood of vipers, how can you who are evil say anything good? For the mouth speaks what the heart is full of. You snakes! You brood of vipers! You shut the door of the kingdom of heaven in people's faces. You yourselves do not enter, nor will you let those enter who are trying to. How will you escape being condemned to hell? Woe to you, teachers of the law and Pharisees, you hypocrites! You clean the outside of the cup and dish, but inside they are full of greed and self-indulgence. Blind Pharisee! First clean the inside of the cup and dish, and then the outside also will be clean. (Matthew 12:34, 23:13, 25–26, 33)

However, he seemed to contradict himself by disclaiming any judgment of the world.

> You judge by human standards; I pass judgment on no one. (John 8:16) But if I do judge, my decisions are true, because I am not alone. I stand with the Father, who sent me. (John 8:50)

> I am not seeking glory for myself; but there is one who seeks it, and he is the judge. (John 12:47)

> If anyone hears my words but does not keep them, I do not judge that person. For I did not come to judge the world, but to save the world. (John 12:47)

He refused to condemn a woman taken in adultery and saved her from execution by stoning when he admonished her accusers, "Let any one of you who is without sin be the first to throw a stone at her" (John 8:1–11). But he seemed to break his own rule by displaying considerable anger at the money changers and sellers of doves at the temple: "And Jesus went into the temple of God, and cast out all them that sold and bought in the temple, and overthrew the tables of the money changers, and the seats of them that sold doves, And said unto them, It is written, My house shall be called the house of prayer; but ye have made it a den of thieves" (Matthew 21:12–13). This sounds pretty judgmental to me. I wonder how Jesus would react to modern megachurches that are tax-exempt money pits.

Later, the scripture says he will return as judge and ruler of the world for a thousand years (Acts 10:42, Revelation 20:6). These scriptures illustrate the danger in proof texting the Bible as they seem to say opposite things. So preachers choose the scriptures that support their objectives and omit the others. All in God's will, of course.

Some Jews, including the twelve apostles he handpicked from among his disciples or chose one by one (Matthew 4:18–2, Luke 6:13,) wanted to identify Jesus as the Messiah who was to inaugurate God's reign and free the Jews at last from their incessant captivities. He admitted to being Messiah, but he disappointed them by declaring, "My kingdom is not of this world." The disappointment of the Jews erupted after he was crucified in a revolt against Rome in 69–70 CE that included destruction of the temple. They revolted again in 132–135 CE that dispersed the Jews, as Emperor Hadrian barred them from Jerusalem to root out Jewish nationalism upon the defeat of "false Messiah," Simon Bar Kokhba, who led the revolution. There is no explanation of how he could conscript, equip, train, and support several hundred thousand Jewish troops without Roman awareness.

Jesus described the Kingdom of God (a.k.a. Kingdom of heaven) variously as a place one could enter, a place one could see, and something that is "within you and among you" (KJV). The word "kingdom" appears 162 times in the New Testament. There is general agreement among scholars that the term used by Jesus himself would have been "Kingdom of God." Matthew's use for the term Kingdom of heaven is generally seen as a parallel to the usage of Kingdom of God in Mark and Luke's gospels. While the concept of "Kingdom of God" has an intuitive meaning to lay Christians, there is hardly any agreement among theologians about its meaning in the New Testament. The phrase "Kingdom of God" is interpreted in different ways to fit the theological agenda of those interpreting it. Some scholars see it as a Christian lifestyle, some as a method of world evangelization, some as the rediscovery of charismatic gifts, others relate it to the world to come.

Through his teaching, Jesus explained the nature of that kingdom, who will enter, and how one lives in it. This he did with thirty-seven parables (an earthly story to convey a heavenly meaning, metaphors in the Synoptic Gospels that use an unrelated word to describe another, except for the Gospel of John, which contains none). They both revealed the Kingdom of heaven to those designated to invest in it and hid the truth to those unwilling to invest in it and to those who were not called to receive him. Some Jews were destined to reject it. "A stone that causes people to stumble and a rock that makes them fall. They stumble because they disobey the message—which is also what they were destined for" (1 Peter 2:8). He acknowledged it takes the faith of a child to enter the Kingdom of God (Mark 10:15).

His other teachings pointed beyond the law of Moses to a higher righteousness that demanded nonretaliation to injustices and love for enemies. Through his healing miracles, his exorcisms, forgiveness of sins, and the love he demonstrated to outcasts, the power of faith, plus the inspired teaching that overruled the law, he brought into reality the presence of God's power in the lives of his followers. His selection of disciples was a call to enter God's Kingdom and to take up their cross and follow him. But more than that, the special group of twelve apostles, a motley crew of fishermen, tax collectors, and publicans, became the nucleus of the Church as the new people of God. With Jesus, the Kingdom of God, the new reign of God, began. For those who believed in him, he promised nothing less than everlasting life:

> God so loved the world he gave his only son so that whoever believes in him will not perish but will have everlasting life. (John 3:16)

> He said to Martha, sister of Lazarus whom he was to raise from the tomb, "I am the resurrection and the life. The one who believes in me will live, even though they die, and whoever lives by believing in me will never die. Do you believe this? Yes, Lord, she replied, I believe that you are the Messiah, the Son of God, who is to come into the world." (John 11:25–27)

Jesus consistently spoke of himself as the "Son of Man," a somewhat enigmatic figure who combined humility and suffering with divine power and future majesty. His demeanor and authoritative pronouncement indicated that he was the "suffering servant of the Lord" spoken of in Isaiah 40–55. Wherever he went, he aroused great interest, engendered hope, and stirred up opposition from the temple leaders, called the Sanhedrin, who were threatened by his popularity and criticism of their hypocrisy apparently.

His Sermon on the Mount or on the plain stands as the supreme disclosure of a new covenant with the people of God because he taught, not as the scribes, but as "one having authority" (Matthew 5–7, Luke 6:17–49). The Sermon on the Mount is generally considered to contain the central tenets of Christian discipleship. Unlike the scribes and Pharisees who could only quote scriptures, Jesus created scriptures. Like this one, called the Golden Rule: "So in everything, do to others what you would have them do to you, for this sums up the Law and the Prophets" (Matthew 7:12). Actually, this instruction appears in the works of Confucius in the fifth century BCE. It appears to be projecting your personal desire onto someone else. What if you are a masochist and want others to put you into chains and beat you with a strap for sexual pleasure? Should you do that unto others? If you are a drug addict and want others to feed your habit, should you do that unto others? Perhaps the negative version works better: "Don't do to others what you wouldn't want to have done to yourself." You see, it gets complicated when you think about it.

It would be more useful to do unto others as they would have you do unto them—up to the limits of health, safety, and legality. Buying drugs for addicts is not helpful even though it may sustain friendships or enable family members. After basic needs of food, clothing, shelter, and reproduction, people want social connections and self-fulfillment. They also need praise, empathy, attention, and acceptance (PEAA), a little of which goes a long way to help make friends. If you do the opposite, you may create an enemy. If everyone gave to others what they want, life would be much different, but good judgment must prevail to maintain your personal boundaries. This obviously would not apply to criminal or abusive behaviors. Apply PEAA to desirable behaviors and ignore the rest.

Jesus did not eliminate suffering. His famous set of blessings, the Eight Beatitudes, on the poor, peacemakers, the mourning, the persecuted, and the rejected meek among the suffering masses stands in stark contrast to the "celebrity preachers" who proclaim the desire of God is for everyone to enjoy peace, health, wealth, and happiness—especially them. They just ignore the troublesome scriptures in the Bible that would not support their purpose, which is to fill stadiums with people looking for a magical blessing and to maintain their standard of living. You can fool all the people some of the time and some of the people all the time by claiming the Gospel solves all your problems—and people keep buying those lottery tickets. Never mind reality. There is something unhealthy when people put a religious celebrity on a pedestal. Jesus declared, "But you are not to be called 'Rabbi,' for you have one Teacher, and you are all brothers. And do not call anyone on earth 'father,' for you have one Father, and he is in heaven. Nor are you to be called instructors, for you have one instructor, the Messiah. The greatest among you will be your servant. For those who exalt themselves will be humbled, and those who humble themselves will be exalted" (Matthew 23:8–12).

Jesus found his teaching and his lifestyle troublesome for the religious leaders of Jerusalem. They often questioned his authority and even his sanity. The late American theologian William James wrote, "Healthy-mindedness is inadequate as a philosophical doctrine, because the evil facts which it positively refuses to account for are a genuine portion of reality; and they may after all be the best key to life's significance, and possibly the only openers of our eyes to the deepest levels of truth" (*The Variety of Religious Experience*, 1902, 2016). For James, the practical consequences of saintliness are pleasure in sacrifice, strength of soul in a blissful equanimity free from anxieties, a withdrawal from the material world, and charity and tenderness to those most people would naturally disdain. One is reminded of Mother/Saint Teresa who devoted her life to the homeless wretches of Calcutta. When someone asked if her work was just a drop in the bucket, she replied, "It is more like a drop in the ocean, but without it, the ocean would be less." Perhaps Jesus had similar feelings about his mission as he said, "The harvest is plentiful, but the workers are few" (Matthew 9:7).

During his short three-year ministry, Jesus performed many miracles, from changing water into wine to healing blind people, the lame, demon possessed, and even raising two people from the dead. These actions, combined with his radical teaching about the kingdom of God, branded him as anathema to the Jewish religious rulers who saw him as a mortal threat to their social status and control. They responded by attacking his lifestyle and engaging with their Roman occupiers to remove him from the scene before the people could see the potential impact of his life in changing the social environment of their place and time.

Jesus did proclaim the abundant life, "I am come that they might have life, and that they might have it more abundantly" (John 10:9–11). He also told his disciples, "Truly I tell you, no one who has left home or brothers or sisters or mother or father or children or fields for me and the gospel will fail to receive a hundred times as much in this present age: homes, brothers, sisters, mothers, children and fields—along with persecutions—and in the age to come eternal life. But many who are first will be last, and the last first" (Mark 10:29–31). Notice the promise comes with persecutions. The Old Testament prophet wrote, "Bring to the storehouse a full tenth of what you earn so there will be food in my house. Test me in this, says the Lord. I will open the windows of heaven for you and pour out all the blessings you need" (Malachi 3:10). Such scriptures have been used to promote "prosperity gospel," which implies God provides wealth and happiness for those who ask and believe and donate—blatant proof texting.

Apparently, Jesus was not referring to the standards of the world because he said, "The spirit gives life, the flesh counts for nothing" (John 6:63). "Anyone who loves their life will lose it, while anyone who hates their life in this world will keep it for eternal life" (John 12:25). In fact, he said if you get all your rewards on earth, there will be fewer to hope for in heaven—twelve times in the book of Matthew. He turned social values upside down by claiming the first shall be last and the last shall be first (John 20:16). He said to be the greatest one must be the servant of all, and he washed the apostles' feet to demonstrate. He said one should forgive those who harm us seventy-seven times if they ask for it and to forgive everyone before you pray as a precondition for response (Matthew 18:22, Mark 11:25). And we should love our enemies and do good to those who despitefully harm us (Matthew 5:43–45). And he told his disciple one must leave everything, hate his whole family, and take up a cross and follow him (Luke 14:26). Nothing is there about being healthy, wealthy, and happy. Can you see what happens when you proof text or cherry-pick the scriptures?

Unfortunately, his instructions in passivism, obedience to governors, poverty, submission, service, unconditional love, forgiveness, and sacrifice are as anathema to many Christians today as they were then to religious leaders and the wealthy gentry. Origen, the first major Christian theologian, wrote that although wars between non-Christians may be necessary, it is impossible for Christians to fight in a war—even in self-defense—without compromising the faith. It is interesting that soldiers on both sides in a war pray to the same God for victory—and we even have religious chaplain services in the military. It is said that General George S. Patton ordered his chaplain to write a prayer for him asking God for clear weather for a crucial battle in WWII, and it worked. "Military chaplains" is an oxymoron, as would also be "Christian soldiers" for sure. However, someone said there are no atheists in foxholes.

Islam teaches a different view. The Quran tells Muslims to fight for Allah and, win or lose, they will be given a mighty reward. "Therefore, let those fight in the way of Allah, who sell this world's life for the hereafter; and whoever fights in the way of Allah, then be he slain or be he victorious, We shall grant him a mighty reward" (4.74). So if both sides are loyal to their dogma, Muslims win, and Christians lose in a war. Passive Muslims and militant Christians both would seem to be hypocrites, as they were in the Crusades during the tenth and eleventh centuries when the Church tried to regain possession and control of the holy land, which failed. You likely won't hear such things discussed in churches very much, especially those that have members who are in the military. When they proclaim the goal of being like Christ, they scarcely know what that really means. Neither did the first twelve apostles, who swore they would follow him no matter what because they did not anticipate the cross was coming. But when Jesus said there is no greater love than giving your life for your friends, I doubt he was referring to warfare (John 15:13). Perhaps he was referring to his own destiny on the cross. Of course, we will never know for sure.

Jesus spent most of his short (three-year?) ministry around the Sea of Galilee, but he felt the compulsion to go to Jerusalem for a final ministry around the temple at the center of Judaism. He rode into the city on a donkey (as was predicted in Zechariah 9:9), but he was acclaimed and cheered as a conquering hero. After several confrontations in the Temple with the religious authorities, in which he even more critically undercut the authority of the religious establishment. Judas Iscariot, one of the twelve, was recruited by the high priests to identify Jesus for them in fulfillment of Old Testament prophecy in payment of thirty pieces of silver (Zechariah 11:13). After a mock early morning trial before King Herod and Pontius Pilate, the Roman governor (details of which are quite muddled because the Jews did not have authority to execute him), he was nevertheless condemned to die by crucifixion on the day after Passover. Jesus knew his suffering was inescapable because that is why he came into the world, but nevertheless he prayed to the Father, "If it is possible, let this cup pass from me, but let your will be done" (Matthew 26:42). Beaten and humiliated, Jesus was forced to carry his own cross to the hill, Golgotha, outside the city wall, where he was executed by Roman guards, crying out in shame, agony, and defeat, "My God, why have you forsaken me?" Judas was so remorseful he threw the money back at the priests and went and hanged himself (Matthew 27:5) or he used the money to buy a field where he fell headlong, his body burst open, and all his intestines spilled out (Acts 1:18). One or other of these accounts may be true, but not both. The apostles chose a replacement to join them by casting lots, who was named Matthias, but we hear nothing more about him (Acts 1:26).

Though Jesus was guilty of no civil crime, he infuriated the Jewish temple leaders by violating the Sabbath, healing sick people, and forgiving their sins, so they trumped up charges that he was claiming kingship and powers of God. The Romans were nervous about revolutionaries and reluctantly gave in to the wishes of the riotous religious tribunal, the Sanhedrin, who felt threatened by Jesus's popularity and his authority. When Pilate the Roman governor, asked if he was proclaiming himself a king as the Jews alleged, Jesus replied, "Yes, but my kingdom is not of this world" (John 18:33–38). He also admonished Pilate by saying, "You have no power over me not given to you from above. Do you think I cannot call on my Father, and he will at once put at my disposal more than twelve legions of angels?" (Matthew 26:53). But that was not part of his destiny. The charge written on the cross was "King of the Jews." His accusers railed, "We have no king but Caesar." Thus, the charge under which Jesus was executed was that of inciting sedition. The Romans wanted to show the Jews what happens to anyone flaunting their rule, and the Jewish Sanhedrin wanted to purge a threat to their control and authority. The scripture says some of the Jews acknowledged their responsibility. "When Pilate saw that he was getting nowhere, but that instead an uproar was starting, he took water and washed his hands in front of the crowd. I am innocent of this man's blood, he said. It is your responsibility! All the people answered, His blood is on us and on our children!" (Matthew 27:11–26). That is why the Jews are reviled to this day by some Christians.

However, Jesus saw his death as part of God's predestined plan to make a new covenant with humanity, replacing the old covenant under the laws of Moses, and thus to save the human race from eternal punishment if they were destined to believe in him and accepted his sacrifice as vicarious atonement for their sins in breaking the law (Mark 14:24, John 3:16, Romans 10:9). But he also said no one can come to him unless the Father calls or enables them. (John 6:65). Thus began a debate about free will and predestination that is unsettled to this day. You can find arguments for both as well as compatibility theories in scriptures. Here is a scripture that declares both sides in the same place. "(*Predestination*) Now listen, you who say, Today or tomorrow we will go to this or that city, spend a year there, carry on business and make money. Why, you do not even know what will happen tomorrow. What is your life? You are a mist that appears for a little while and then vanishes. Instead, you ought to say, If it is the Lord's will, we will live and do this or that. As it is, you boast in your arrogant schemes. All such boasting is evil. (*Free will*) If anyone, then, knows the good they ought to do and doesn't do it, it is sin for them" (James 4:13–16). The debate seems to be over free will or God's will. But if you ask whether the Bible supports belief in free will or predestination, the answer is yes.

Decision Making

Acceptance of the Bible and Jesus as Messiah/Savior requires a decision of most importance because your decision could determine where you spend eternity, if there is one. Decision processes could be a separate study. It gets complicated. Some modern experiments in neurology seem to show the brain makes decisions before we are conscious of them, but if that applies to all decisions is unknown. In his blog "The High Price of Free Will," Dr. Robert M. Price says, "Neuroscience reveals that when we (think we) make a decision, it is actually the conscious awareness of that choice having been made just beforehand deeper in the physical brain. We are, in short, taking orders, playing a role in a play we did not author—and (maybe) with *no* author" (*Zarathrustra Speaks*, July 2018). Some decisions must be made so quickly you don't have time to think about it while others take longer. But perhaps neither results from free will, even though we can believe it does. People choose the options that favor the perceived benefits more than the burdens, even though unconsciously.

This process can be likened to an iceberg where most of it is submerged in the subconscious mind. The top must go where the bottom takes it. But the benefits always must be presumed to outweigh the burdens in all decisions, even if unconsciously. And these can include matters of the heart as well as the mind, or maybe also hormones. One extreme example is that of Nadya Suleman, the "Octo single mom" who had fourteen children, eight of them in one birth after she had six others, all by in vitro fertilization. Another example: An army veteran adopted five children with Down syndrome after her own daughter was born with the birth defect. And another: At his age of eighty, actor Bill Cosby was convicted of sexual crimes that he committed many times during his years prior to his very popular and lucrative career. One more: President Richard Nixon won forty-nine states for his second term, but he was forced to resign after he was threatened with impeachment for obstruction of justice.

Consider the decision to speed up to get through the caution light before it turns red and risk getting a ticket or come to a screeching stop and risk getting tail-ended. A baseball batter facing

> a 90mph fast ball has .63 second to decide to swing and to complete that action, but the fans in the stands can take their time deciding to be there. First, they must decide to go, then get a ticket, dress and show up, etc. Experiments show that once they become conscious, decisions seem to be controllable – fans could buy a ticket and decide not to go. But is that really free will or predetermined by all the decisions that came before including invention of the game of baseball and construction of the stadium? The late great boxing champion Muhammad Ali had an uncanny ability to avoid the attempted punches of his opponents and to retaliate instantly with deadly accuracy. But first he had to decide to be a boxer and to train intensely after his parents decided to birth him and their parents birthed them and so on back to the first parents.
>
> Ben Franklin explained his decision method of drawing two columns on a sheet of paper and labeling them "for" and "against." He would list all the motives for any decision on each side and assign personal values to each one—say, on a scale of ten—then total up each side to make the best choice after he had subtracted the items of equal value on each side. He observed, "The longer I live, the more convincing proofs I see of this truth—that God governs in the affairs of men." Perhaps there are no mistakes, only choices and consequences. So as you read this book, you will have to decide, "What has that got to do with me?"

As inevitable and horrible as it seemed on the cross, his death was not to be the end of the story for Jesus. He predicted, "A time is coming and in fact has come when you will be scattered, each to your own home. You will leave me all alone. Yet I am not alone, for my Father is with me" (John 16:32). However, he felt forsaken by God while hanging on the cross. His disciples did flee and returned to their homes, but some of his women disciples went to the tomb on the morning of the third day on the first day of the week and found it empty. They also saw a messenger or an angel or two men who said, "He is risen!" Another group of disciples claimed that he appeared among them at various times and places and ate with them and instructed them to spread his message throughout the world. In one account, he appeared to them through locked doors. Therefore, they knew that Jesus had been vindicated by God; death could not hold such a predestined life. "For this cause I was born, and for this cause I have come into the world" (John 33:18:37).

Moreover, Jesus promised to return and take the elect with him to live forever in heaven. "I go to prepare a place for you…in my Father's house are many rooms." The timing of these future events was known only to the Father as not even the Son was given those secrets, except they were to occur within the present generation. Meantime, they were to take the message to all nations of the world—God sent his only son into the world to save the sinful people whom he had created, but only if they were given the faith to believe it and were called for his purpose (John 3:16, 6:44, 65, Romans 8:28). He promised to send the Holy Spirit after he was gone to empower them. The Holy Spirit is referred to in third person as "he" throughout scriptures. Therefore, the latter notion that the Father, Son, and Holy Spirit exist as three in one is flimsy at best.

As his disciples pondered all the events that had taken place (Luke 24), things that Jesus had said and done began to fall into place. When they experienced the power and presence of the Holy Spirit after his resurrection, their disbelief changed into conviction, and their despair was transformed into joyful hope of his imminent return. They believed that God's reign would come during their generation after all to those who believed and "were called according to his purpose."

The Early Church: 30–60 CE

After the four gospels, the rest of the New Testament traces the history of the spread of faith in Jesus Christ and draws out some of the implications of the life, death, and the resurrection of Jesus for the life and faith of the earliest Christians.

The book of Acts describes the spread of the gospel (i.e., the "good news" about Jesus) from the religious center at Jerusalem to Rome, the center of the empire's political power. However, it is neither the acts of all the apostles nor all the acts of any apostle. After the disciples had waited fifty days until the Jewish festival of Pentecost for the power Jesus promised, they suddenly were "filled with the Holy Spirit," the very presence and power of God. This presence and power of God in the person of the Holy Spirit like "tongues of fire" enabled people who had gathered from all over the world to hear the good news about Jesus in their own languages: "Repent, for the Kingdom of Heaven is at hand." The scattering of languages at Babel was thus reversed, and a new unifying force of God was at work in the world. Everyone could now be told through interpretation in their own tongue that God had made this Jesus who was crucified both Lord and Christ, and those who believed were baptized into a new universal fellowship, that is, saved from their enslavement to sin. The laws of the old covenant with Moses had been replaced by the laws of a new covenant through Christ. "For this reason, Christ is the mediator of a new covenant, that those who are called may receive the promised eternal inheritance—now that he has died as a ransom to set them free from the sins committed under the first covenant." (Hebrews 9:15) Note that the promise is to those who are called. This idea appears throughout the New Testament.

The incipient movement was condemned by Rome and endured persecution without retribution by the traditional Jews who feared the loss of their control and benefits of temple priesthood. The rapid advance of the gospel from Jerusalem to the neighboring provinces was counterbalanced by opposition from Orthodox Jews. There were imprisonments and even martyrdom. Stephen, one of the new group of leaders called deacons, was the first who was stoned to death. Saul of Tarsus, a Jewish-born Roman citizen and Pharisee, was a witness and concurred in the execution. He also went door to door searching out Christians and having them imprisoned. The advancing Gospel of Jesus centered first on the Apostle Peter and then on Saul renamed Paul, who was accosted and converted in a flash of light by the very Jesus whom he was persecuting. In obedience to the heavenly vision and the working of the Holy Spirit, Peter baptized the first Gentile converts and thus opened the door to the whole non-Jewish world, much to the chagrin of Orthodox Jews who demanded that they should be circumcised and obey the laws of Moses to enter the community of faith.

Paul declared his mission thus: "I only know that in every city the Holy Spirit warns me that prison and hardships are facing me. However, I consider my life worth nothing to me; my only aim is to finish the race and complete the task the Lord Jesus has given me—the task of testifying to the good news of God's grace" (Acts 20:23–24). He redefined the people of Israel, those he calls the "true Israel" and the "true circumcision" as those who had faith in the heavenly Christ, thus excluding those he called "Israel after the flesh" from his new covenant (Galatians 6:16, Philippians 3:3, Hebrews 8:7–13). He also held the view that the Torah law given to Moses was not valid after Christ came so that even Jews are no longer under the Torah, nor obligated to follow the commandments given to Moses (Galatians 3–4), which caused a rift with the Jewish Christians. Thus, Paul was the great Apostle to the Gentiles who, through his three missionary journeys, threw open to the world the gates of reconciliation to God in a new covenant between Christ and those called to declare him Lord and Savior. By using the modern names, we can easily trace his missionary journeys.

Using Antioch in Syria, where they were first called Christians, as his home base, his first trip took him to south-central Turkey. In a second trip, starting from Antioch, he traveled from one end of Turkey to the other and then crossed over to northern Greece (Macedonia) and ended at Corinth in southern Greece. His third missionary journey centered in the city of Ephesus in western Turkey, but also took him again to the churches in Macedonia and Greece. When Paul returned to Jerusalem, he was mobbed by his enemies and imprisoned. After two years in jail at Caesarea, the Roman capital in Palestine, he was sent on a ship to Rome to await trial as a Roman citizen at his request. He finally arrived there after a long voyage, a great storm, and a shipwreck.

The spread of the Gospel of Jesus raised serious questions about God and about the life of faith, as well as practical issues that exercised the Church for a long time: what is the relation of the old people of God, the Jews, to the new people of God, the Christian Gentiles? And what is the relation of the original Jewish Christians to the increasing number of Gentile Christians?

At first, the Church, the believers in Jesus as Lord and Messiah, was simply a sect within Judaism. But as Paul's success among the Gentiles increased, so did the tensions between the traditional Jewish Christians and the new nontraditional Gentile Christians. That is, did a Gentile have to become a Jew and obey the entire Mosaic law to become a Christian? Paul wrote, "If you declare Jesus Christ is Lord and believe in your heart that God resurrected him from death you will be saved" (Romans 10:9). But Jesus had taught, "No one can enter the kingdom of God unless they are born of water and the Spirit" (John 3:5). Then he complicated it even more with this condition: "You will be hated by everyone because of me, but the one who stands firm to the end will be saved" (Matthew 10:22). Are these scriptures mutually exclusive or what?

Scripture reports in Acts 15 that a council was held in Jerusalem in 49 CE, which decided that the Gentile Christians did not have to obey the whole Jewish law in order to be saved or to be Christians. They just needed to avoid blood, eating animals that were strangled, adultery, and even circumcision. Although Christians are freed from the laws of Moses, they are not free from sin under the laws of Christ. Jesus had instructed, "If you love me, keep MY commandments" (John 14:15). Since churches rarely teach the commandments of Christ, the people do not obey them either. Neither do the Orthodox Jews obey the laws of Moses. If they did, the world would be a much different place. If you consider the Bible as the Word of God, there can be found 1,050 commands in sixty-nine categories throughout the New Testament (www.cai.org). Refer to appendix A for a short list. After you read them, you may agree we all are hypocrites.

The book of Acts concludes with Paul proclaiming the new reality of God's reign from his house arrest in Rome, the capital of the empire of his world. Though he was a prisoner facing possible execution, the closing verse of Acts assures the reader that his preaching of the Gospel and the spread of God's Kingdom continued "unhindered." His eventual demise is unknown although second-generation writers claimed he was executed.

The Letters of Apostle Paul: 48–62 CE

A very important part of Paul's ministry were the letters he wrote to the churches he had organized. They are our most direct connection with this great apostle and his leadership in the early church. It is doubtful he had access to any of the Gospels, so there are some conflicts with the teachings of Jesus, but the letters of Paul laid out the main policies and beliefs he instructed the incipient church of Christ.

In his missionary travels, his assignment was to preach first to the Jews in the synagogue and then speak to the Gentiles. Most of these Gentiles (non-Jews) were actually "God-fearers" associated with the synagogue—Gentiles who were attracted to Judaism and who studied the law and worshipped Yahweh, but who were not circumcised and who did not observe the ritual Jewish laws. The integration with such Gentiles and Orthodox Jews would be a problem for all the first-century Christians. After gathering a group of converts and appointing some bishops and deacons, he would move on to other missionary fields. His continuing contacts were by means of letters and personal messengers, sixteen of which are in the New Testament canon.

Because faith in Jesus Christ as savior was a new religion for Jews and a whole new belief for Gentiles, new issues were constantly being raised that Paul needed to explain. The letters traditionally ascribed to the Apostle Paul are Romans, 1 and 2 Corinthians, Galatians, Ephesians, Philippians, Colossians, 1 and 2 Thessalonians, 1 and 2 Timothy, Titus, and Philemon. However, many scholars now hold that 1 and 2 Timothy, Titus, and possibly Ephesians, Colossians, and

2 Thessalonians were written by followers of Paul in his name after his death.

Paul wrote as a missionary pastor theologian. As a theologian, he emphasized implications of the life, death, and resurrection of Jesus for individual persons, for the church as a corporate body, and for history as a whole. He wrote his understanding of faith, hope, and love for the Church, and his hope for a life everlasting. As a pastor, he was concerned with the moral and spiritual life of the Christian church and with church order. The letters are "occasional letters" in the sense that they were written to or for a specific situation, whether in anticipation of or in response to a practical issue regarding faith and life. Paul's letter to the Romans and the post-Pauline letter to the Ephesians are both examples of more general epistles or statements of the Christian faith.

The basic message of Paul's letters is that Jesus is the answer to everlasting life for both Jews and Gentiles. "If you declare that Jesus Christ is Lord and believe in your heart that God raised him from the dead, you will be saved" (Roman 10:9). Not only the pagan Gentiles, but Jews too are alienated from God by sin and are in bondage to the powers of sin and death. Jesus Christ is the God-sent deliverer ("Messiah" is the Hebrew word, meaning "Christ," or in Greek, "anointed one"), God's Son, the Lord of history, the very power and righteousness of God to set creation on the right path toward a new covenant with God. The individual person who identifies with Jesus and personally appropriates what Jesus has done by faith is said to be "saved" from the wages of sin, which is derived from disobedience to the laws of Moses. In Paul's vocabulary, faith means not only belief or assent, but also obedience and trust in the commandments of Christ. He declared a personal relationship with the risen Lord, if only in human imagination. The words in traditional hymns reinforce this imaginary relationship as often as they are sung. Consider this example: "We serve a risen savior, he's in the world today." Or this: "What a friend we have in Jesus, all our sins and grief to bear." Or this: "Oh Lord, you know I have no friend like you. If heaven's not my home then, Lord, what will I do?"

However, Dr. Robert M. Price challenged the description by Paul of the last supper by observing the gospels were not written yet, and he was not an eyewitness. Therefore, Paul's claim to divine inspiration is based on his own imagination, intuition or some oral testimony – most likely the latter. "For I received from the Lord what I also passed on to you: The Lord Jesus, on the night he was betrayed, took bread, and when he had given thanks, he broke it and said, This is my body, which is broken for you; do this in remembrance of me. In the same way, after supper he took the cup, saying, This cup is the new covenant in my blood; do this, whenever you drink it, in remembrance of me. For whenever you eat this bread and drink this cup, you proclaim the Lord's death until he comes" (1 Corinthians 11:23–36, Matthew 26, Mark 14, Luke 22). Since scholars claim the letter to the Corinthians was written before the gospels, the faithful claim Paul must have been writing from some inspired source, or this entry was added later by a scribe who possessed one of the gospels. Moreover, Jesus was addressing the disciples at the table as "you" and not everyone for all time, else he would have said, "This is my body, which is given for everyone who believes in me." But, he didn't say that. The authority of Jesus often was challenged by the Pharisees and the Sanhedrin, but the authority of Paul rarely is questioned in scriptures after his initiation in Jerusalem. Interesting.

Moreover, Paul described himself as one who matured in his faith and ministry as an example to others who are called to a new and challenging way of life. "When I was a child, I talked like a child, I thought like a child, I reasoned like a child. When I became a man, I put the ways of childhood behind me" (1 Corinthians 13:11). He also claimed, "I discipline my body and bring it into subjection, lest, when I have preached to others, I myself should become disqualified" (1 Corinthians 9:27). Nevertheless, he lamented that he still did what he would not and left undone things he should do. "What a wretched man I am! Who will rescue me from this body that is subject to death? Thanks be to God, who delivers me through Jesus Christ our Lord! So then, I myself in my mind am a slave to God's law, but in my sinful nature a slave to the law of sin" (Romans 7:23–25). So it seems that good and evil can coexist even in those called to preach the Word, as evidenced by the sexual scandals among Catholic priests. Modern research indicates criminal behavior is linked to abnormal neuron wiring in the brain, which may account for psychopathic individuals. We each may contain both a Jesus and a devil, and each one must have its day. Hence the populations in prisons. Necessary opposites, for sure, just like up and down, sweet and sour, hot and cold, pain and pleasure, hope and despair, positive and negative, heaven and hell, etc.

Faith like Paul's may be a product of human intuition, what Swiss psychiatrist C. G. Jung (1875–1961) called "active imagination," and he said it is the ability to "see around corners." Dr. Jung would argue that the very idea of god is an archetypal pattern that is preconscious and that is universally present and thriving in the "collective unconscious." That is to say people have an instinctive tendency, desire, or need to believe in such unknowable higher essences as gods and heavens, hell, etc. Albert Einstein said intuition is the basis of all scientific discovery as "the answer comes to you and you don't know how or why." Napoleon said, "Imagination rules the world." Nothing can be created that is not first imagined. Consider these secular examples:

Bill Gates saw the opportunity when he was in college and took action that became Microsoft Inc. Jeff Bezos got the idea for online retailer, Amazon.com, while driving cross country. Danny Thomas got the idea for St. Jude children's hospital while a television star. Mark Zuckerberg got the idea that became Facebook while he was a sophomore in college. Travis Kalanick got the idea for Uber while he was carpooling to work. Elon Musk got the idea for SpaceX rockets to Mars while building Tesla electric cars. Ken Wilber got his ideas about integral psychology while studying biology. Joel Osteen got the idea for his prosperity ministry, with no formal training, after the untimely death of his pastor father. Adolf Hitler got the idea for Nazism after failing as a student of architecture. Joseph Smith Jr. got the idea for Mormonism while treasure hunting in Palmyra, New York. Muhammad got the idea for Islam while meditating in a cave. Kris Kristofferson got the idea for his country music career while studying at Oxford, trying a military career, and flying helicopters for oil companies. Taylor Swift got the idea for music stardom while still a child in Reading, Pennsylvania. Jennifer Lawrence got the idea for her movie career after acting in church plays and dropped out of school at age fourteen. Donald J. Trump got the idea of being president while he was a real estate developer. I don't know where Jimmy Wales and Larry Sanger got their idea for Wikipedia, but I am glad they did.

These celebrity stories illustrate the creative process that works through the subconscious mind of everyone. They are examples of what C. G. Jung called active imagination: "All the works of people (good or bad, important or trivial) originate in their active imagination." The imagination of Jesus suffering, crying out in pain, on the cross to save you from the penalty for your sins is a powerful call to conviction, remorse, and repentance, which are necessary prerequisites to being saved. One might say this book is a product of my creative imagination or intuition, which is a function of my personality. Or maybe you could say it is inspired by God. Thus, the whole New Testament corpus may be imagined by the writers who were not eyewitnesses—and not who the titles imply that they were—copying from each other and the testimony of various oral traditions.

Paul uses several terms to describe that saving action: "justification" means to set in right relation, "reconciliation" expresses the overcoming of alienation, "redemption" carries the idea of deliverance and restoration, and "re-creation" speaks of renewal and newness of life. Newness of life is made possible by the power of the Holy Spirit in both the individual's life and in the Church, and its main manifestation is self-giving love, which is the very nature of God because God is love—except when he is a raging, consuming fire (John 4:8, Hebrews 10:27, 12:29). At the heart of Paul's message was his conviction that Christ is the power of God to set humanity right with God. This justification by grace through faith puts Jews and Gentiles on equal footing so that all alike might be saved on the same basis. Furthermore, Jesus was going to return very soon to redeem all of creation and to restore the reign of God—even within the generation of those presently alive. "But the day of the Lord will come like a thief in the night. The heavens will disappear with a roar; the elements will be destroyed by fire, and the earth and everything done in it will be laid bare" (1 Thessalonians 5:2, 2 Peter: 3:10). "Truly I tell you, this generation will certainly not pass away until all these things have happened" (Matthew 24:34). Since 2,000 years have passed without these things happening yet, some people may claim that the predictions of Nostradamus are more reliable than this.

Other New Testament Letters

In the letters of Paul's followers, matters of church order, proper doctrine, and sound leadership became more important subjects. These letters reflect a church struggling to define faithfulness in an increasingly hostile world dominated by ruthless Roman rulers. They reflect the situation and needs of second-generation (i.e., post-70 CE) Christianity, not those of first-generation (i.e., pre-70 CE) Christian Judaism.

Although these letters claim Paul as author, there is good reason to conclude that they were written by Paul's later followers in his name, that is, pseudepigrapha. These include Ephesians, Colossians, 2 Thessalonians, 1 and 2 Timothy, and Titus. As opposed to the undisputed letters of Paul, these letters are known as the disputed letters of Paul, the deutero-Pauline letters, or the post-Pauline letters.

In these post-Pauline letters, several new challenges faced by the Church are addressed. Specifically, how should the Church understand and deal with the following:

1. The delay of Christ's return?
2. People teaching false doctrine?
3. The needs of the Church for ongoing leadership?
4. An increasingly hostile, sometimes persecuting world?

These letters take a harder line against supposed heretics, and they are more concerned with the institutional and organizational needs of the Church. They reflect a new interest in establishing clear leadership structures in light of the delay of Jesus's return, and they advocate a more conservative ethic, including a much more restricted role for women in the church compared to that enjoyed by first-generation Christianity. For instance, the status of women is presented differently as advocated by Jesus (Luke 7:50, 8:1–3; John 7:53–8:11) and Paul (Romans 16:1–6, 12; Galatians 3:28; Philippians 4:2–3) and that advocated by the post-Pauline letters (Ephesians 5:21–28, Colossians 3:18–19, 1 Timothy 2:8–15). However, the prescribed roles of wives and husbands deserve reconsideration in this day of no-fault divorce and single mothers.

The other letters usually are called the general epistles, which simply designates a miscellaneous category. The book of James, assumed by some scholars to be written by a brother of Jesus, apparently seeks to correct an overemphasis on faith as separate from good works by saying that faith, if it is to have any integrity at all, must be lived in deeds. This later would become a contentious issue in the Reformation.

The book of Hebrews is an anonymous sermon that affirms the superiority of Christ within the Jewish faith and its religious institutions and exhorts believers to a life worthy of Christ's suffering.

First Peter is a beautiful and powerful plea to Christians living under persecution to follow the pattern of the suffering Christ and to realize that they are a chosen race, a holy people.

John's three letters are addressed to churches threatened by the temptation to deny the real humanity of Jesus and to assimilate the values of the world. The author reminds his readers that they have seen and heard the revelation in Christ. First John was also written to encourage and comfort Christians who had just experienced a church split.

Whoever they were, the writers were called to meet the spiritual needs of their generation through the story of Jesus, which definitely worked in their time. Unfortunately, many churches today are so busy with a social and pop-psychology agenda to fill their tax-exempt treasuries; their programs do not provide much in the way of spiritual nurture. This was predicted by Apostle Paul: "For the time will come when people will not put up with sound doctrine. Instead, to suit their own desires, they will gather around them a great number of teachers to say what their itching ears want to hear. They will turn their ears away from the truth and turn aside to myths." Nor do they help carry each other's burdens as did the first church in Jerusalem and Apostle Paul instructed (2 Timothy 4:3–4, Acts 5:1–11, Galatians 6:2). Like modern medical doctors, one must go to churches because they are not going to come to you. I think the professional nurses in the world, Christians or not, deserve much honor for their service to the suffering souls. Response to the call of Christ in faith to serve can be discussed in terms of the personality model developed by Dr. C. G. Jung and expressed in the Myers-Briggs Type Indicator. (Refer to appendix D for more details.)

The Revelation to John

The final book of the Bible is among the strangest and yet most intriguing. It is an apocalypse, a revelation, which uses visions, numbers, and dramatic symbols to picture the ultimate goal of God's action in Christ, that is, a new world totally governed by God and his holy people after the final cataclysm obliterates the enemies of God.

This book, written by Apostle John in exile on the Isle of Patmos, reveals that it is precisely through Jesus's death on the cross and his resurrection (i.e., in his nonviolent resistance to the powers of evil) that Jesus proved ultimately victorious. The lion, the root of David—symbol of God's victorious Messiah—proves to be none other than the slain but victorious Lamb of God who holds the scroll of human destiny in his hand and thus determines the fate of all humans and human institutions. Therefore, even small groups of believers who are facing harassment and martyrdom can know that they are on the winning side, that all evil and wickedness has already been vanquished on the cross and ultimately will be destroyed.

God's revelation of Jesus Christ to John is thus designed to provide encouragement and strength to Christians facing the hostility of a world convinced that power politics or the evil one controls the events of history. Even more, it encourages Christians living in seven cities of the province of Asia to wake up and to reject the temptation to assimilate to the lifestyle and values of the Roman Empire (with its worship of the emperor) and to embrace a consistent and watchful allegiance to Christ alone.

At the end of it all at some future time known only to God, his enemies all will be destroyed, and Christ will reign supreme with his people in a new Jerusalem within a new heaven and a new earth for eternity.

Commentary

Doubt is not a pleasant condition, but certainty is absurd.

—Voltaire

Lord, make me an instrument of your peace Oh, Master, grant that I may never seek so much to be consoled as to console, to be understood as to understand, to be loved as to love with all my soul.

—St. Francis of Assisi

Lord, give me that pacific mind which spreads Thy peace throughout humankind and knits them all in one.

—Wesley, 1958–70

Modern life is an unending source of anxiety and sadness occasionally pierced by momentary joy and hope.

—Anonymous

Without freedom of thought there can be no such thing as wisdom and no such thing as public liberty without freedom of speech.

—Ben Franklin

As I wrote in the preface, which I hope you read, I am not a professional religious scholar, so I cannot assume to know anything but a very small fraction of all there is to know about the Bible.

However, I can read. No matter what translation is used, the basic story of the Bible is there for anyone to read as well. To read it in sixty different English translations or to search for a topic or scripture of interest, visit www.biblegateway.com. Also, as noted, I am given to rely on the New International Version since it seems to be well developed by many scholars and enjoys wide acceptance among many churches. This commentary may seem to be redundant, but that must be necessary to supplement the history above with information that you don't get in church.

For those who may wish a complete Bible commentary by a renowned scholar, I recommend the books by Dr. Robert M. Price, PhD. For other related work, I recommend the books by Dr. Bart D. Ehrman, Bishop John Shelby Spong, and Dr. Michael Shermer listed among the references. But fair warning: these scholars and others show that human analysis using professional methods of literary critique gives a different perspective on the Bible, one that is based not on faith, but on reason. My commentary is based on many years of study using the *Thompson's Chain Reference Bible* as my primary resource. The basic issue I struggle with is how faith and reason can be merged for a better application of the Bible scriptures to contemporary understanding of the world. Someone said that with faith no proof is necessary, and without faith no proof is sufficient. But that is not good enough for me. So I begin with the end in mind.

Many writers have discussed the various contradictions in the Bible, where it says one thing in one place and something apparently different in another place. A search on Amazon.com for "Bible contradictions" produces a list of 240 books, many of them by biblical scholars of renown. It is easy to deconstruct the Bible, but reconstructing it is more difficult—like trying to put Humpty-Dumpty back together again. It is a challenge I am not well qualified to tackle, but I seem to have no other choice. People have been martyred for less, but here I stand. I must learn and share what I learn. Avoiding these issues or relying on proof texting merely challenges the faith of believers and fuels arguments of skeptical critics. Some apologists try desperately to reconcile variations in scriptures by claiming it is all a matter of translation or interpretation, and if you think there are contradictions, you just don't understand. I taught Sunday school under that pretense for twenty years, but it finally required a truthful commentary after I read it for myself. I had to find a way of accommodating the realities of scriptures with my personal reality of living on earth in my time and place. Otherwise, I would have to become an atheist like some other Christian scholars have done.

Possibly the most basic conflict is the sign of Jonah that Jesus said would be evidence of his coming as Messiah. "Now the LORD provided a huge fish to swallow Jonah, and Jonah was in the belly of the fish three days and three nights" (Jonah 1:17). "For as Jonah was three days and three nights in the belly of a huge fish, so the Son of Man will be three days and three nights in the heart of the earth" (Matthew 12:40). If Jesus died on Friday afternoon and was resurrected on Sunday morning, the first day of the week, this sign was invalid. Scriptures refer to his resurrection as "on the third day" (Matthew 17:23, 20:19, Luke 18:33, 24:7). Moreover, the various descriptions in the Gospels of what happened on the day of resurrection, when the tomb was found to be empty and the body of Jesus was missing, are inconsistent. The scriptures do not say when he actually was removed or left the tomb. The only common elements are the tomb was empty, and the body of Jesus was gone. Similarly, the accounts of his birth are different in the only two gospels that describe it, but the scriptures contain some basic elements, that is, God sent his only son into the world to be crucified to save some people, whom he has preselected, from eternal suffering in hell for being the sinners he created them to be, by making laws he knew they would disobey. What is wrong with this picture?

For many Christians, the conflicting details do not matter. But there are serious apparent contradictions that impact the basic dogma of Christianity, and these cannot easily be reconciled. Skeptics claim such differences in scriptures prove the Bible is not the Word of God, and the purists find ways of accommodating them to suit their a priori conclusions, often by proof texting, that is, cherry-picking scriptures out of context. This battle has been going on since the first century, so perhaps it is necessary, or it would be resolved by now. I do not intend to support one side or the other but merely to point out the various conflicting issues in certain scriptures and let you draw your own conclusions. If they are avoided and not settled, churches become little more than tax-exempt social service clubs—beneficial as they may be. My comments are those that come to mind after reading the Bible for myself, as I was apparently destined to do. I realize others may focus on different issues, and I have no comment about that either up front. I will have my say at the end in the conclusions. I will write as I am given, so let's begin at the beginning.

The Old Testament

You may recall the first book of the Bible, Genesis, begins with God creating the heavens and the earth and all that dwell therein. Scripture says it was all "good." He also created the first man and woman, Adam and Eve, and placed them in a Garden of Eden and gave them dominion over it. He permitted them to eat the fruit of every tree except the tree of knowledge of good and evil, lest they surely die. Note that the first humans were vegetarians. But Eve succumbed to the persuasion of the serpent, ate the fruit of the tree, and induced Adam to eat it also. Thus, the woman was the first sinner and not the man. They immediately lost their innocence, so God drove them out of the garden lest they might also eat of the tree of life and become immortal like the gods. The man had to work the soil to obtain food and the woman had to suffer in childbirth while the serpent crawled on his belly. They produced two sons, Cain and Abel. Cain killed Abel in a jealous fit because God preferred the blood offering of Abel to the farm produce of Cain. God did not punish Cain, but protected him and made him the father of cities. The mother of cities is not explained, but there had to be some incest going on. We will come back to this scenario later. The Bible says in those early days there were giants upon the earth who mated with the women and created some form of hybrid being: "There were giants in the earth in those days; and also after that, when the sons of God came in unto the daughters of men, and they bare children to them, the same became mighty men which were of old, men of renown"

(Genesis 6:4). Some people wonder if these giants were alien visitors from another world. Believe it or not.

The story of the relationship between God and his rebellious humans goes on to the point where God decides the only solution is to start over. So he chooses one family for their best behavior and instructs the father, Noah, to build a water craft large enough to hold a pair of every living land creature with provisions for forty days to survive a massive flood he sends to wipe out all the land life plus another forty days to await its abatement. Obviously, the marine life survived as is. The interesting thing about this story is, how do you support the carnivores and herbivores for so long without their natural habitat plus stock enough supplies to maintain them all after the flood until a new harvest could be restored? I keep wondering about those carnivores. What did they eat? And how did he round up those elephants from India? How did he collect and store all the feed for the herbivores? The food supplies must have had to last much longer than eighty days because the earth was void after the flood. When you think about all the life-forms down to snakes, flies, and ants, etc., that must have been quite a menagerie. Only God could pull that one off.

However, the real story is in the behavior of Noah and his family of three sons and their wives after the flood. It seems like nothing really was gained as they just processed the same human DNA as before and kept on misbehaving as people apparently must do. We could discuss the incest that was needed to repopulate the human race, but we will not go there. After all, there were only Noah, his wife, three sons, and their wives. The righteous man proceeded to plant a vineyard—where did he get the seeds?—and proceeded to get drunk. I guess he thought he deserved it (Genesis 9:20–23).

The descendants of Noah disappear into history as they exit the stage and roam about repopulating the earth. He is replaced in the story with another righteous man named Abram and renamed Abraham. He and his wife Sarah are passed their childbearing years in their eighties, but God still promises to make him the father of nations and to provide for them as needed in a land of milk and honey while defending them from all their enemies. He will be their only god, and they will be his people if they obey his conditions for the covenant. The problem is that Abraham got impatient as years passed and still no heir. So his wife, Sarah, persuades him to father a child with her handmaid, Hagar, which produces a son named Ishmael. When the promised son, Isaac, is born, they reject Ishmael and send him and his mother out into the desert with a bag of bread. However, God promises to take care of them and to establish his descendants as a great nation also. Some scholars think Ishmael is the ancestor of Muhammad and, thus, the patriarch of Islam, which is no friend of the Jews.

Abraham proves his loyalty and obedience to God by demonstrating his willingness to sacrifice his son, Isaac, as a blood offering, but he is relieved of this gruesome task. Isaac proceeds to produce a son named Jacob who steals the birthright from his elder twin brother, Esau, by staging a daring scheme to impersonate him concocted by his mother. Jacob proceeds to father twelve sons with two wives and several concubines, the youngest of whom and most loved is Joseph. When the jealousy of his brothers cannot be contained, they sell him off to a traveling caravan into Egypt, telling their father he was eaten by wild animals. Joseph is enslaved by the chief bodyguard of the king of Egypt, titled Pharaoh, and enjoys living in the palace until the queen falsely accuses him of attempted rape, which lands him in prison. While there, he demonstrates a skill of interpreting dreams for the jailers. When Pharaoh has a troubling dream, Joseph is called to interpret and warns the king of a coming famine throughout the area that will last seven years after seven years of plenty. Appropriately impressed, the king puts Joseph in charge of accumulating stores during the fat years in preparation for the coming lean years. When they come, Egypt is in the enviable position of having grains to sell to their neighbors who were not so forewarned or prepared. The star of Joseph rises, and he is second in power in Egypt only to Pharaoh.

As things happen, what comes around goes around, and the family of Joseph still living back in Canaan face starvation unless they can buy grain from Egypt. There follows some emotionally charged reunions in which the family of Jacob, now called Israel, totaling some seventy souls including in-laws and grandchildren, is able to migrate and live in the land of Goshen at the pleasure of Pharaoh in gratitude to Joseph for saving his bacon, so to speak—plus, making him very rich. Joseph forgave his brothers for selling him off because it was necessary to eventually put him in a place where he could save his family from starvation. They become prosperous and contented there being able to own land and to conduct business and multiply—emphasis on multiply. Eventually, Joseph died and succeeding pharaohs who forgot about him proceed to enslave the tribe now called Hebrews and engage them in making bricks for the king's many official construction projects. Did I say they multiplied? In fact, the pharaoh attempted to curtail their expansion by ordering the killing of all male infants, but the midwives claimed the Hebrew women gave birth too quickly to prevent the increasing population. This goes on for like 400 years. It seems that God just forgot about his chosen people and the covenant he made with Abraham. Maybe he was busy making other worlds.

To avoid the genocide of newborn males ordered by Pharaoh, a young Hebrew Levite mother, Jochebed, hides her infant boy in some weeds near the palace. She sees her wishes granted when he is discovered by a royal servant and is taken into the court to be raised as a prince named Moses. He grows into a mighty warrior. Although he does not know he is one of them, he feels sorry for the lot of the Hebrews, and when he spots a slave master beating one of them, he ups and kills the slave master. The word gets around, and Moses splits to go into exile to avoid his certain arrest and gets married with children and works as a shepherd for his father-in-law. His life settles into a comfortable routine. Finally, after 400 years in captivity, God hears the cries of his people in Egypt and decides to appoint a deliverer to liberate them. He chooses to recruit Moses, the murderer, by calling to him through a burning bush that really is not burning. Moses is very reluctant because he knows from experience the power of Pharaoh and is somewhat lacking in the speech department. So God appoints his brother, Aaron, as spokesperson, and Moses agrees to leave his family and take on the impossible task of freeing the people of Israel. When he asks God who he should say has sent him when the Israelites ask, the reply is, "Tell the people I AM has sent you" (Exodus 3:14).

So when I feel anxious and want to experience God, I repeat this mantra: "I Am Here and Now." It works to calm me down and helps to create serenity in the midst of chaos that is life. Many Christians are so busy doing things and talking on their cell phones they do not take enough time for personal contemplation and spiritual nurture. Whether from Buddhism or psychology, evidence indicates that spending time each day in quiet meditation is good for you. Living in the past invites depression, and living in the future invites anxiety. One can learn to live in a mindfulness mode, concentrating on the here and now because that really is all we have for sure. (For more on this, refer to my book *Better Living, Better Dying*.)

The Bible says that God hardened the heart of Pharaoh so he would not let the Hebrews leave. So Moses was given the power to bring a dozen plagues down on Egypt in escalating fashion that did not convince Pharaoh until the last one finally got his attention. This seems to be a rather harsh way to free the Jews from captivity, but it shows the power and will of God to visit suffering upon his creation. First, he uses Joseph to influence the Pharaoh of Egypt to shelter the Hebrews from famine, then he arranges for them to become captive slaves, and 400 years later, he stops Pharaoh from freeing them and brings national grief upon the people: "Then the LORD said to Moses, Go to Pharaoh, for I have hardened his heart and the hearts of his officials so that I may perform these signs of mine among them" Exodus 10:1). In his ultimate sign, God killed all the firstborn sons of Egypt including that of Pharaoh. The firstborns of the Jews were saved by putting a stroke of animal blood on the lintels above the doorways, hence their celebration of the "Passover" to this day. However, after relenting, Pharaoh changed his mind and pursued the several hundred thousand Jews into the sea, which Moses had parted so they could get through, and lost all his army including horses and carriages when it flooded back over them. Thus endeth the story of Pharaoh. All in God's will, of course.

To assure himself that all the senior generation who feared attacking the inhabitants of the promised land all were dead, the

Bible says Moses led the Jews around in the Sinai Peninsula for forty years before they finally made it back to the holy land (Exodus 16). This is surprising since the trek could be taken in less than two weeks according to modern-day travelers, even on foot. Life was hard in the desert, and the people harped at Moses and wished they had never left Egypt where they at least had the basic needs of life—and reproduction. "Why did you bring us up out of Egypt to this terrible place? It has no grain or figs, grapevines or pomegranates. And there is no water to drink!" (Numbers 20:5) So God intervened and supplied food from heaven while Moses struck a rock and obtained water. However, the people lost their faith in Yahweh, the God of Moses, and began to worship a golden calf made from melting down their jewelry. At this revolting development, Moses went up Mount Sinai to consult with God and was given the Ten Commandments as the token of covenant that God had made with Abraham. Remember him? When Moses returned down from the mountain, he found the people having a major party worshipping a golden calf they made from melting down their jewelry. He got so mad he threw the tablets down and broke them and so had to go back to get a replacement set. In addition to the Ten Commandments, Moses compiled a comprehensive set of laws concerning how the Jews should live, 613 in all, comprised of do's and don'ts. They were very harsh, like stoning a woman found in adultery and cutting off the hands of a thief, demanding an eye for an eye and an ear for an ear, etc.

Thus, it was that the Hebrews, now called Jews, made it to the edge of the land of Canaan that God had promised to their ancestor, Abraham. Remember him? Moses was not permitted to enter the promised land as he died when his assignment was completed, and the torch was passed on to his aide, Joshua. The only problem was the land was occupied by six tribes who had to be removed to make place for the Jews. The Bible says that God ordered Joshua to invade the land and to kill all the men, women, and children: "My angel will go before you and bring you to the Amorites, Hittites, Perizzites, Canaanites, Hivites, and Jebusites; and I will wipe them out" (Exodus 23:23–30). It seems this was not done in a single battle but occurred over some time. There are some discussions among historians and archaeologists if this is true or not, but that is what the Bible says.

The book of Joshua describes the many battles fought by Joshua to carry out the promise of God to give the land to Israel: "Joshua took all these royal cities and their kings and put them to the sword. He totally destroyed them, as Moses the servant of the Lord had commanded. Yet Israel did not burn any of the cities built on their mounds—except Hazor, which Joshua burned. The Israelites carried off for themselves all the plunder and livestock of these cities, but all the people they put to the sword until they completely destroyed them, not sparing anyone that breathed. As the Lord commanded his servant Moses, so Moses commanded Joshua, and Joshua did it; he left nothing undone of all that the Lord commanded Moses" (Joshua 11:12–15). So much for the commandment "thou shall not kill." The Bible says that peace settled in the land because there were no more indigenous people to kill—ergo genocide.

After the Jews settled into their holy land, other battles ensued with their neighbors, and they became jealous of those who were ruled by kings. Enter the story of a prophet, Samuel. Prophets are defined as the spokesmen of God. Actually, the Bible lists some sixty different prophets, but only a few are useful in this story. Samuel was opposed to kings and tried to persuade the people that the benefits, if any, were not worth the burdens, but he was finally forced to give in to their demand. Samuel searched through the tribes and chose Saul as the first king of Israel. Saul was a competent administrator and warrior, but he tended to disobey God, especially when it came to the genocide of enemies of the Jews that he conquered. Although his son, Jonathan, was in line to be king, Samuel sought out a different replacement and discovered David, the youngest son of the house of Jesse. David was made a ward of Saul and was raised in the palace as a prince next to the king's son, Jonathan, who became his best friend.

At one point in a battle with the Philistines, David slays their warrior giant, Goliath, with a stone from his slingshot and becomes an instant hero. David was made a ward of Saul and was raised in the palace as a prince next to the king's son, Jonathan, who became his best friend. David became a warrior more successful than Saul in battles, which upset Saul more than a little as the people cheered, "Saul has slain his thousands, but David has slain his tens of thousands." Saul would get so depressed that he tried to kill David with a spear, but missed—several times. At such times, David would play his harp and sing to the king, which would calm him down. But eventually, both Saul and Jonathan were killed in a battle so David could become the second king of Israel. It really is an interesting story and would make a good movie.

David was a great king, but like Saul, he was flawed also. When he saw Bathsheba, wife of Uriah the Hittite and battle commander, bathing on a rooftop, David had an affair with her and got her pregnant. In an attempt to hide the consequences, David ordered Uriah home from battle and encouraged him to sleep with his wife, but Uriah declined since his soldiers did not have such opportunities with their wives. Then David had Uriah placed in front of the lines in battle to get him killed. As punishment, the first son of David with Bathsheba was born dead, and so the second son, Solomon, became the next king of Israel. The crowning achievement of David was to conquer the Jebusites and occupy the city of Jerusalem, making it the capital of Israel and the city of David. The Bible says Jesus was descended from King David. Therefore, the ancestor of Jesus Christ, the Messiah, was an adulterer and murderer. God works in mysterious ways.

Solomon was an even greater king than David who conquered many enemies and carried off many wives and concubines. He built the first temple in the middle of Jerusalem and placed in its center the Holy of Holies, the Ark of the Covenant, the original gold-leaf box containing tablets of the Ten Commandments given to Moses. By then, a priestly class was formed from the tribe of Levites to maintain and administer sacraments in the temple. Solomon also was a man of letters and seems to have been interested in contemplating the nature of life in general. Despite being the richest man in the world, he was unhappy and concluded, "Everything is utterly meaningless… With much wisdom comes much sorrow, with much knowledge comes much grief" (Ecclesiastes 1:18).

After King Solomon and his son, the oppressive Rehoboam, there followed the reigns of many kings over Israel. They were involved with continuous interior uprisings and battles at a time when arms consisted of swords, spears, and bows and arrows. The Bible says nothing about what was done with all the dead soldiers and the wounded. It would seem the kings had forgotten the commandment given by Moses, "Thou shall not kill." Most of the kings did something displeasing to the Lord and were replaced again and again. Only two found favor with God; Hezekiah at the end of the 700s BCE and Josiah about seventy-five years later were the two kings noted for their faithfulness and reforms.

It seemed that the chosen people of God just could not get their act together. If they were not worshipping idols and living in debauchery, they were fighting wars with their enemies, of whom there seems to be no end. If there is one word to describe the history of Israel, it is "war." This when the weapons were swords, spears, and pikes. Through it all, God remained behind the scenes, apparently busy doing other things among the many other nations of the world and the wide variety of life species that occupied planet earth—like developing the metamorphosis of caterpillars turning into butterflies and fruit pollination by honey bees, and the tree frog in the Arctic that freezes to death each winter and thaws out to revive in the spring. This part of the Bible story in the Old Testament trails off with the invasion by Babylonia in 586 BCE and the exile of the Jews who never really were able to completely reconstitute the nation of Israel that God promised to Abraham until President Harry Truman did it with the aid of the United Nations in 1948.

Considering the travail, pathos, and suffering of the chosen people, one may conjure three possibilities regarding God: (1) he wanted to remove their suffering but he could not, (2) he could have removed their suffering but he chose not to, or (3) he was the one causing all their troubles. The same goes for the rest of us. A case for the latter conclusion is found in the scriptures themselves that you probably do not get in church. The Bible claims that God does not just allow bad things to happen as some theologians claim, but he actually causes them: "The Lord kills and makes alive; The Lord makes poor and makes rich; He brings some low and lifts some up" (1 Samuel 2:6–7); "I make peace and create evil/calamity. I, the Lord, do all these things" (Isaiah 45:7). In this context, the Hebrew word for "evil" is translated elsewhere in the Bible as spoiled, bad, adversity, trouble, sinful, misfortune, calamity, so take your pick: "When a disaster comes to a city, has not the Lord caused it?" (Amos 3:6); "Though you build your nest as high as the eagle's, from there I will bring you down, declares the Lord" (Jeremiah 49:16, Obadiah 1:4); "Who has spoken and it came to pass, unless the Lord has commanded it? Is it not from the mouth of the Most High that good and bad come?" (Lamentations 3:37–38); "When times are good, be happy; but when times are bad, consider this: God has made the one as well as the other" (Ecclesiastes 7: 14). The Quran says the same thing to Muslims: "No calamity comes, no affliction occurs, except by the decision and preordainment of Allah" (S:64.11). You probably don't get that in church.

Considering his penchant for hurting his own creation, it may be appropriate to feel angry at God whenever he imposes suffering on your life—and maybe even rage if the impact is major. That is the way I felt when my wife died at age fifty-two, ending our plans for spending time together on our bucket list after the kids were raised. I have lived with posttrauma shock ever since. If it was God's will for her to die like that, it must also be his will for me to hate it like I do. God has some serious explaining to do. The thing is at their time in history, the writers could not envision a god above the one they had created in their own image. But, now we can.

So then we have the story of Job, in which God permits Satan to destroy his family, wealth, and even his health just to win a wager that he would not lose his faith or his devotion. It is an interesting story that some apologists claim shows the permissive will of God. After losing everything at the whim of Satan, Job lives up to his role and refuses to blame God. "At this, Job got up and tore his robe and shaved his head. Then he fell to the ground in worship and said: Naked I came from my mother's womb, and naked I will depart. The Lord gave and the Lord has taken away; may the name of the Lord be praised. In all this, Job did not sin by charging God with wrongdoing" (Job 1:20–22). God reprimands Job for questioning his intention by reminding him of who created whom and declares the created cannot question the creator. In the end, Job regains all he lost without explaining how his wife could replace all their kids, but some scholars say this was added much later to make the story end in happier ever after. If there is a lesson for us in here someplace, what is it? In my opinion, it just illustrates the confusion in the Bible about God and the danger of proof texting scriptures to prove one side or the other. But if you do not proof text, the opposing scriptures create confusion about its theology. There are many other books in the Old Testament worth reading that are beyond this commentary, so I will leave them to your extra study. But beware of the possible challenges to your belief.

The New Covenant

The main theme of the New Testament is that the old covenant given to the Jews through Moses was replaced with a new covenant founded on acceptance of Christ as Lord. At the "last supper" with the twelve apostles before he was crucified, scripture declares, "After the supper he took the cup, saying, This cup is the new covenant in my blood, which is poured out for you" (Luke 22:20). "Christ is the mediator of a new covenant, that those who are called may receive the promised eternal inheritance—now that he has died as a ransom to set them free from the sins committed under the first covenant" (Hebrews 9:15). Scriptures describe the converts to the new covenant among the Jews and Gentiles as "those who are called" several times. "And we know that in all things God works for the good of those who love him, who have been called according to his purpose. For those God foreknew he also predestined to be conformed to the image of his Son, that he might be the firstborn among many brothers and sisters." (Romans 1: 6-7, 8:27-29, Galatians 1:6, 1 Peter 2:9, Jude 1:1)

After a period of silence for some 400 years, the Bible begins a new era in the life of God's chosen people called the New Testament. Throughout their troubled history, the Jews yearned for some miracle that would produce a leader capable of routing all their enemies and installing them in the land of milk and honey they thought was promised to them by God. In the play *Fiddler on the Roof*, the Jewish patriarch, Tevye the Dairy Man, laments, "Lord, I know we are the chosen people, but sometimes couldn't you just choose somebody else?" He did have a point. There were people developing cultures and nations throughout the continents of Asia, Africa, Europe, and the Americas who apparently did not figure into the plan of God. Moreover, archeologists have discovered the Etruscan extinct culture that occupied the area of Italy in 600–100 BCE that became the center of Rome 500 years before Christ. It seems the God of the Old Testament was only interested in his relationship with the chosen people of Israel and he could not care less about all the others in his creation.

Numerous times in the New Testament, reference is made to a scripture in the Old Testament that some scholars assume is a prophecy of the coming Messiah, that is, the deliverer of the Jewish nation and the savior of humankind. The prophets Isaiah and Zechariah seem to predict such a savior. Isaiah 53 presents a promised one who would die for the sins of God's people and rise again. Isaiah 50:6 accurately describes the beating that Jesus endured. Some Christians believe that this verse refers to the birth of Jesus as the Messiah: "For a child will be born to us, a son will be given to us; And the government will rest on His shoulders; And His name will be called Wonderful, Counselor, The Mighty God, The Everlasting Father, The Prince of Peace" (Isaiah 9:6). Christian authors have interpreted Zechariah 9:9 as a prophecy of an act of messianic self-humiliation. "Rejoice greatly, O daughter of Zion! Shout in triumph, O daughter of Jerusalem! Behold, your king is coming to you; He is just and endowed with salvation, Humble, and mounted on a donkey, Even on a colt, the foal of a donkey." Subsequently, Jesus entered Jerusalem on a donkey. Zechariah 12:10 predicts the piercing of the Messiah, which occurred after Jesus died on the cross. The prophet Isaiah, addressing King Ahaz of Judah, promises the king that God will destroy his enemies. As a sign that his oracle is a true one, Isaiah predicts that a "young woman" or "virgin" (*almah*) will shortly give birth to a child named Immanuel (meaning God with us) and that the threat from the enemy kings will be ended before the child grows up (Isaiah 7:14).

The Gospel of Matthew presents Jesus's ministry as largely the fulfilment of prophecies from Isaiah (Mathew 1:23). In the time of Jesus, however, the Jews of Palestine no longer spoke Hebrew, and Isaiah had to be translated into Greek and Aramaic, the two commonly used languages. In the original Hebrew of Isaiah 7:14, the word *almah* meant a young woman of childbearing age who had not yet given birth and who might or might not be a virgin, and the Greek translation rendered *almah* as *parthenos*, which meant the Greek word for "virgin." Scholars agree that *almah* has nothing to do with virginity, but many conservative American Christians still judge the acceptability of new Bible translations by the way they deal with Isaiah 7:14.

The virgin birth is found only in the Gospels of Matthew and Luke; there is no reference to the birth of Jesus in Mark's Gospel or the Gospel of John, nor in the epistles of Paul, who says that Jesus was "born of a woman" without mentioning that the woman was a virgin. The books of Matthew and Luke trace the genealogy of Jesus back to Abraham and Adam in both directions respectively, one directly through Joseph and the other through Joseph as the husband of Mary. These lists are identical between Abraham and David (except for one), but they differ almost completely between David and Joseph. Matthew gives Jacob as Joseph's father, and Luke says Joseph was the son of Heli. Luke lists seventy-five generations backward from Jesus Son Man back to Adam Son of God. Attempts at explaining the differences between the genealogies have varied in nature. Much of modern scholarship interprets them as literary inventions. Purists will say they are validation of the prophecy; and skeptics may say it shows the Messiah is based in murder (Cain, David), adultery (Abraham, David), and fraud (Jacob.) Loyalists claim this genealogy shows that God can use flawed people for his purpose.

Scripture says after his temptation during forty days in the wilderness following his baptism by John, Jesus returned to Nazareth where he read in the synagogue from the scroll of Isaiah: "The Spirit of the Lord is on me, because he has anointed me to proclaim good news to the poor. He has sent me to proclaim freedom for the prisoners and recovery of sight for the blind, to set the oppressed free, to proclaim the year of the Lord's favor. Then he rolled up the scroll, gave it back to the attendant and sat down. The eyes of everyone in the synagogue were fastened on him. He began by saying to them, Today, this scripture is fulfilled in your hearing" (Luke 4: 18–21). The issue of Old Testament prophecy is more complex since the Jewish leaders rejected Jesus as Messiah, but this introduction will have to suffice.

It is worth noting the difference between Christian and Jewish interpretations of such scriptures. Judaism holds that the Messiah has not yet arrived, namely, because of the belief that Jesus did not fulfill the prophecies so the Messianic Age has not started yet. People of the Jewish faith do not regard any of these as having been fulfilled by Jesus and in some cases do not regard them as messianic prophecies at all. Jews believe that the Messiah will completely change life on earth and that pain and suffering will be conquered, thus initiating the Kingdom of God and the Messianic Age on earth. Christian belief varies, with one segment holding that the Kingdom of God is not worldly at all because Jesus said, "My kingdom is not of this world," while another believes that the Kingdom is both spiritual and of this world in a Messianic Age where Jesus will rule on the throne of David. Most Jews hold that the Kingdom of God will be on some new earth and the Messiah will occupy the throne of David. Jews hold that life on earth after Jesus has not changed profoundly enough for him to be considered the Messiah.

Some Christians (in particular, evangelicals) believe that it is both and claim that the Kingdom of God is spiritual and within right now, and it will be physical and outward at the triumphant return of the Messiah. While Christians have cited the prophecies referencing the life, status, and legacy of Jesus, Jewish scholars maintain that these passages are not messianic prophecies and are based on mistranslations/misunderstanding of the Hebrew texts. Be that as it may, I will comment on the scriptures as they exist in the New International Version (NIV) without attempting to judge or to confirm or deny any other aspect of them.

The four books of the New Testament called gospels (good news) and the letters from Paul of Tarsus provide the basis for

Christian living. However, they were written several decades after the events by different authors at different times from differing sources, mostly oral storytellers, so it is not surprising that different stories are told differently in the various books. I leave the details of who wrote what when and where up to the scholars to focus on the words of the scriptures and those alone.

The basic dogma of Christian churches as I learned it is as follows:

* Humankind inherited a sinful nature from the disobedience of the first man.
* Their sin consigns them to eternal death in agony of hell without some external intervention.
* God so loved humankind that he provided his son as a divine intervenor and a martyr to save his people by suffering the punishment for their sins who was Jesus bar Joseph bin Nazareth.
* Belief in Jesus as Lord and Savior is the only way to personal redemption and everlasting life, provided you obey all his commandments and are called for his purpose.
* Eventually, he will return to earth to vanquish all opponents and to set up an eternal kingdom (a.k.a. dictatorship) sans Satan and his angels, which will have no end.
* The Church of Jesus Christ was established to provide a place of refuge in life and a means of communicating this dogma to everyone in the world.

Now let's discuss how the New Testament validates this dogma—or not. If the Bible is the Word of God, every word carries equal authority.

The Sinful Nature of Mankind

First, the problem of sin. The Bible does not define sin per se, but it certainly has a lot to say about it. Sin is mentioned 951 times in the Old Testament and 413 times in the New Testament. There are too many entries to discuss all of them, so a few will have to suffice. Paul writes that "all have sinned and fallen short of the glory of God" (Romans 3:23). "Therefore, just as sin entered the world through one man, and death through sin, and in this way death came to all people, because all sinned" (Romans 5:12). On the other hand—there is always another hand—the Bible says nothing about the sin of disobedience by Adam being passed to his own son, Cain, who murdered his brother Abel. In fact, Cain was protected and made the father of cities. There is no explanation for the mother of cities. Moreover, when Jesus healed a man blind since birth and was asked who sinned, the man or his parents, Jesus replied, "Neither this man nor his parents sinned because the blindness was caused by God to show his power in healing" (John 9:3). Healing cannot come except from sickness, hence sickness is necessary for healing. Further, Jesus said he did not come to call the righteous, but sinners to repent. "It is not the healthy who need a doctor, but the sick. I have not come to call the righteous, but sinners" (Matthew 9:13, Mark 2:17). So it appears that some people may not need a savior.

Paul locked sin with the laws of Moses active at that time among the Jews. "Therefore no one will be declared righteous in God's sight by the works of the law; rather, through the law we become conscious of our sin… For if those who depend on the law are heirs, faith means nothing and the promise is worthless, because the law brings wrath. And where there is no law there is no transgression… To be sure, sin was in the world before the law was given, but sin is not charged against anyone's account where there is no law" (Romans 5:13); "For all who rely on the works of the law are under a curse, as it is written, Cursed is everyone who does not continue to do everything written in the Book of the Law. Clearly no one who relies on the law is justified before God, because the righteous will live by faith" (Galatians 3:10–12). Jesus said of the Jews, "If I had not come and spoken to them, they would not be guilty of sin; but now they have no excuse for their sin" (John 15:22). Thus, it seems before the laws were given to Moses there was no condemnation of sinners; where there is no law, there is no lawlessness. And it seems that Jesus said ignorance of the law is an excuse. Or maybe not. No one is deemed to be ignorant of the principles of the moral law, which are written in the conscience of every human being. People all over the world—advanced and primitive—seem to know and accept that certain behaviors including murder, adultery, rape, robbery, perjury, and fraud, etc., are just wrong and our system of laws recognizes that fact.

Paul wrote many specific instructions in various letters that expand on the law in the new covenant, principally discussed in the letters to Romans and Galatians, plus Hebrews. The phrase "the law" occurs 266 times in the New Testament, 50 times in Romans. One such is this: "Therefore no one will be declared righteous in God's sight by the works of the law; rather, through the law we become conscious of our sin" (Romans 3:20). The matter of accommodating the Mosaic laws with the new covenant of Christ, justification by faith and not works, takes up many scriptures in the New Testament and provides grist for continuous discussions. However, the opinions of Paul can be compiled in a summary form. They are too lengthy to insert here, but they are discussed in appendix B for further understanding. A complete discussion of the Mosaic law and Christianity would require another book.

Further, Jesus admonished the disciples for preventing little children to come unto him because he said, "Let the little children come to me, and do not hinder them, for the kingdom of God belongs to such as these. Truly I tell you, anyone who will not receive the kingdom of God like a little child will never enter it" (Matthew 19:14). So children cannot be born sinners to make this work. Some churches set an arbitrary age after which children are confirmed to accept Christ. Finally, sin seems to come in two forms—one deadly and one not. "If you see any brother or sister commit a sin that does not lead to death, you should pray and God will give them life. I refer to those whose sin does not lead to death. There is a sin that leads to death. I am not saying that you should pray about that. All wrongdoing is sin, and there is sin that does not lead to death" (1 John 5:16–17). The Catholic Church separates venial sins from mortal sins. Venial sin, that is, forgivable sin, is a lesser sin that does not result in a complete separation from God and eternal damnation in hell as an unrepented mortal sin would. A venial sin involves a partial loss of grace from God. A mortal sin in Catholic theology is a gravely sinful act, which can lead to eternal damnation if a person does not repent of the sin before death and do the required penance. The current Catholic teaching was formalized at the sixteenth-century Council of Trent. The Bible also says all sins can be forgiven except one. "Anyone who speaks a word against the Son of Man will be forgiven, but anyone who speaks against the Holy Spirit will not be forgiven, either in this age or in the age to come" (Matthew 12:31–32). Yikes!

Eternal Punishment

Now, as to eternal punishment for the confusing aspect of sinning, the Bible says many things, "Do not be afraid of those who kill the body but cannot kill the soul. But I will show you whom you should fear: Fear him who, after your body has been killed, has authority/power to throw you, body and soul, into hell. Yes, I tell you, fear him" (Matthew 10:28, Luke 12:5); "The Lord will judge his people. It is a dreadful/fearful/terrifying thing to fall into the hands of the living God" (Hebrews 10:30–31). One needs faith to fear the Lord. It also is a sobering thought to realize that each day is one more and one less of your life. Necessary opposites, for sure. Be careful what you do with them: "The wages of the righteous is (eternal) life, but the earnings of the wicked are sin and death" (Proverbs 10:16); "If your right eye causes you to stumble, gouge it out and throw it away. It is better for you to lose one part of your body (and go to Heaven) than for your whole body to be thrown into hell" (Matthew 5:30); "And if your right hand causes you to stumble, cut it off and throw it away. It is better for you to lose one part of your body than for your whole body to go in to hell" (Matthew 18:7–9). If taken literally, such instructions could produce many disabled Christians. Punishment is not avoided in this world either. "Yet he does not leave the guilty unpunished; he punishes the children and their children for the sin of the parents to the third and fourth generation"

(Exodus 34:7). But wait, "Whoever does not love does not know God, because God is love" (1 John 4:8). Apparently, his love does not extend to sinners. But Apostle Paul says it does. "But God demonstrates his own love for us in this: While we were still sinners, Christ died for us" (Romans 5:8).

Dereliction of charity also can get one into the molten pits of hell. Jesus told the parable of a king and his stingy servants thus: "The King will reply, Truly I tell you, whatever you did for one of the least of these brothers and sisters of mine, you did for me. Then he will say to those on his left, depart from me, you who are cursed, into the eternal fire prepared for the devil and his angels. For I was hungry, and you gave me nothing to eat, I was thirsty, and you gave me nothing to drink" (Matthew 25:40–42). Similarly, giving a tithe is not enough. "Woe to you, teachers of the law and Pharisees, you hypocrites! You give a tenth of your spices—mint, dill and cumin. But you have neglected the more important matters of the law—justice, mercy and faithfulness. You should have practiced the latter, without neglecting the former" (Matthew 23:23, Luke 11:42). "Religion that God our Father accepts as pure and faultless is this: to look after orphans and widows in their distress and to keep oneself from being polluted by the world" (James 1:27). "There is neither Jew nor Gentile, neither slave nor free, nor is there male and female, for you are all one in Christ Jesus… Carry each other's burdens, and in this way you will fulfill the law of Christ. If anyone thinks they are something when they are not, they deceive themselves" (Galatians 3:28, 6:2). *Islam has made charity a compulsory aspect of its dogma, requiring Muslims to donate 2.5 percent of income as aid to the poor in the form of a tax.*

You won't find many churches preaching these scriptures or giving charity a very high priority among their social ministries. But they usually convene annual fund-raising campaigns. This is unfortunate because it seems the early church was a community that served each other's personal needs as well as their spiritual needs, which no longer is a mission of many Christians. Consequently, social support has been picked up by various government agencies at the expense of taxpayers. I don't think it was intended to be that way. Perhaps family charity does exist among some Christian communities as with the Amish, Mennonites, and possibly Mormons.

The Bible seems to indicate some people are destined for hell. God "hardens the heart of whomever he chooses" (Romans 9:18). "Enter through the narrow gate. For wide is the gate and broad is the road that leads to destruction, and many enter through it. But small is the gate and narrow the road that leads to (eternal) life, and only a few find it… Not everyone who says to me, 'Lord, Lord,' will enter the kingdom of heaven, but only the one who does the will of my Father who is in heaven. Many will say to me on that day, 'Lord, Lord, did we not prophesy in your name and in your name drive out demons and in your name perform many miracles?' Then I will tell them plainly, 'I never knew you. Away from me, you evildoers'" (Matthew 7:13–23). Jesus described the Kingdom of God (a.k.a. heaven) in terms of parables (metaphors using one word for another) that he explained to the disciples, but not to the critical Jews lest they believed, repented, and were redeemed (Matthew 10:13–15). The Bible says it was God's will for the Jews to reject Jesus as Messiah and were destroyed by Rome because their eyes and ears were closed so they would not repent and be saved, and *that was their destiny* (Isaiah 6:9–10, Matthew 10:13–15, Mark 4:10–12, 1 Peter 2:8). In fact, Apostle Paul wrote that about everyone: "For God has bound everyone over to disobedience so that he may have mercy on them all" (Romans 11:32). All the sixty English translations on www. Biblegateway.com say essentially the same thing. In other words, it appears that God made laws so there would be sinners so he could choose to save some of them from their sins, but not all.

In contrast, one commenter wrote, "As Christians, we will never be punished for sin. That was done once for all. There is now no condemnation for those who are in Christ Jesus" (Romans 8:1, Galatians 5:19–21). Because of the sacrifice of Christ, God sees only the righteousness of Christ when he looks at us. Our sin has been nailed to the cross with Jesus, and we will never be punished for it. Consequently, just as one trespass resulted in condemnation for all people, so also one righteous act resulted in justification and life for all people (Romans 5:15–18).

This scripture may be the basis for those Christians who claim "once saved, always saved." That may be all well and good for born-again Christians who commit sins, but it provides no comfort for those who do not get the message and are lost in their sins. Could it be if you do not know about the law of sin and death you cannot be made responsible for your actions? But in modern jurisprudence, ignorance of the law is no excuse. There are no speed limits in Montana, so no one can be arrested for speeding. Laws are only as effective as they can be enforced, so if everyone breaks it, does that mean the law is invalid, like those 55 mph speed limits? In fact, Apostle Paul says that where there is no law, there is no transgression (Romans 3:20, 4:14–15). Thus, if there were sinners among the Hebrews before the laws of Moses, they receive no condemnation.

The commenter continues,

> The sin that remains in our lives, however, does sometimes require God's discipline. If we continue to act in sinful ways and we do not repent and turn from that sin, God brings his divine discipline to bear upon us. If he did not, he would not be a loving and concerned father. Just as we discipline our own children for their welfare, so does our Heavenly Father lovingly correct His children for their benefit. Hebrews 12:7–11 tells us, "As you endure this divine discipline, remember that God is treating you as his own children." Whoever heard of a child who was never disciplined? It is written in Proverbs, spare the rod and spoil the child. If God doesn't discipline you as he does all of his children, it means that you are illegitimate and are not really his children after all. Since we respect our earthly fathers who disciplined us, should we not all the more cheerfully submit to the discipline of our Heavenly Father and live forever? No discipline is enjoyable while it is happening—it is painful! But afterward there will be a quiet harvest of right living for those who are trained in this way.

The debate over this doctrine continues. Every promise of salvation in the scripture has a condition attached. If we fulfill the conditions, the promises are ours—if not, maybe not. For example, we read in Colossians 1:21–23: "And you, who once were alienated and enemies in your mind by wicked works, yet now He has reconciled in the body of His flesh through death, to present you holy, and blameless, and above reproach in His sight *if indeed you continue in the faith*." In 1 Timothy 1:19, Paul refers to some who, by rejecting a good conscience, had made a shipwreck of their faith—possibly not once saved, always saved, that is, backsliding: "Now, brothers and sisters, I want to remind you of the gospel I preached to you, which you received and on which you have taken your stand. By this gospel you are saved, *if you hold firmly to the word I preached to you*" (1 Corinthians 15:1–2). In Hebrews 3:12–14, we are warned: "Beware, lest there be in any of you an evil heart of unbelief in departing from the living God; but exhort one another daily, lest any of you be hardened through the deceitfulness of sin. For we have become partakers of Christ "if we hold the beginning of our confidence steadfast to the end." Apostle Paul laid down many rules for living for Gentiles who accepted Christ. It seems that faith alone is not enough; you must work at it too, else you could fall into the threat of backsliding. (Refer to appendix B.)

Clearly, this is another example of ambiguity and opposing scriptures in the Bible, making it subjected to proof texting if not totally reviewed. Again, the question to ask is this: What has that got to do with me? Which leads into the next Christian assumption that scriptures present Jesus Christ as the only way to salvation and escape from the eternal punishment that all sinners must endure unless they accept him as Lord and Savior.

Jesus as Messiah

Children are taught in Sunday school to memorize the basic tenet of the faith: "God so loved the world that he gave his only begotten son so that whoever believes in him will not perish but will have everlasting life" (John 3:16). Jesus said, "For my Father's will is that everyone who looks to the Son and believes in him shall have eternal life, and I will raise them up at the last day" (John 6:40). Apostle Paul wrote, "Christ is the culmination of the law so that there may be righteousness for everyone who believes. "If you declare with your mouth that Jesus is Lord and believe in your heart that God raised him from the dead you will be saved" (Romans 10:9). "My dear children, I write this to you so that you will not sin. But if anybody does sin, we have an advocate with the Father—Jesus Christ, the Righteous One. He is the atoning sacrifice for our sins, and not only for ours but also for the sins of the whole world. We know that we have come to know him if we keep his commands." (1 John 2:1)

Such scriptures may imply that people have a choice and can use free will to accept or reject the Savior. However, Jesus also plainly states, "No one can come to me unless the Father calls/enables them" (John 6:44, 65). "I am the way, the truth and the light, no one comes to Father but through me" (John 14:6). Jesus also said in Luke 10:22, "And no one knows who the Father is except the Son and those to whom the Son chooses to reveal him." After Peter declared he was the Messiah, Jesus said, "This was not revealed to you by flesh and blood, but by my Father in Heaven" (Matthew 16:17). Jesus told his disciples, "You did not choose me, I chose you." Apostle Paul also considered himself and the church at Ephesus among those chosen by Jesus: " In him we were also chosen, having been predestined according to the plan of him who works out everything in conformity with the purpose of his will" (Ephesians 1:11). Such scriptures seem to nullify the concept of free will, do they not? They also illustrate the folly in proof texting the Bible. They also show that opposing scriptures create conflicts and ambiguities.

Some scriptures seem to claim that Jesus was God: "In the beginning was the Word and the Word was with God and the Word was God" (John 1:1); "I and the Father are one…anyone who has seen me has seen the Father" (John 14:9); "no one has ever seen God, but the one and only Son, who is himself God and is in closest relationship with the Father, has made him known" (John 1:18); and "I and the Father are one" (John 10:30).

But other scriptures quoting Jesus do not support that contention: (John 14:10, 28) "The words I say to you I do not speak on my own authority. Rather, it is the Father, living in me, who is doing his work: for the Father is greater than I"; (John 5:37) "and the Father who sent me has himself testified concerning me"; (John 6:46) "no one has seen the Father except the one who is from God; only he has seen the Father"; (John 8:38) "I am telling you what I have seen in the Father's presence, and you are doing what you have heard from your father"; (John 5:30) "by myself I can do nothing; I judge only as I hear, and my judgment is just, for I seek not to please myself but him who sent me"; and (John 14:30–31) "I will not say much more to you, for the prince of this world is coming. He has no hold over me, but he comes so that the world may learn that I love the Father and do exactly what my Father has commanded me."

In addition, when Jesus faced the suffering of the cross, he prayed to God: "My Father, if it is possible, may this cup be taken from me. Yet not as I will, but as you will" (Matthew 26:39). And while hanging on the cross, he cried out, "My God, why have you forsaken me?" (Matthew 27:46). This hardly is the voice of God speaking to himself. Jesus is referred to as the "Son of Man" eighty-six times in the four Gospels; each time, it is stated in third person as referring to himself in the editorial sense. Jesus is referred to as the "Son of God" thirty-four times in the four Gospels, each time in the third person by the writer, except when he said, "I am God's Son" in the first person (John 10:36). However, Jesus does seem to accept the title of Messiah (Matthew 16:16–20, Mark 8:28–30). When Pilate asked him if he were a king, Jesus replied, "My kingdom is not of this world." (John 18:36) The argument over whether Jesus is God or not began with the first Christians and goes on to this day. All in God's will, of course.

The Plan of Salvation

As to the plan of salvation, it gets very confusing. Apostle Paul of Tarsus wrote, "If you declare that Jesus Christ is Lord and believe in your heart that God raised him from the dead, you will be saved" (Romans 10:9). If taken alone as proof texting, this scripture seems to say it all, and nothing more is required to have eternal life. But wait, he also wrote, "No one can say Jesus is Lord except by the Holy Spirit" (1 Corinthians 12:3). Jesus said, "Very truly I tell you, no one can enter the kingdom of God unless they are born of water and the Spirit" (John 3:5). Jesus also declared in Mark 15:16, "Whoever believes and is baptized will be saved, but whoever does not believe will be condemned." However, Jesus never explained this scripture, so different interpretations of it have been proposed and adopted by various churches—although belief and baptism both seem to be mutually required. Some claim total immersion is required to wash away all sins, and others believe limited sprinkling will do the job.

Common dogmas say that sinners must accept Jesus as savior to be saved, and sinners must go through the narrow gate to enter the Kingdom of God, of which he is the gatekeeper. But there is a catch. "No one knows the Son except the Father, and no one knows the Father except the Son and *those to whom the Son chooses to reveal him*" (Matthew 11:27, Luke 10:22). Jesus also said, "No can come to me unless he is called/enabled by the Father" (John 6:65). To his disciples, he said, "You did not choose me, but I chose you and appointed you so that you might go and bear fruit—fruit that will last" (John 15:16). Are these conditions both/and or either/or? Do we have free will or not? The Bible does not give a clearer solution, so it is open to many different interpretations. Christian baptism is conducted many different ways and "born of the water and the Spirit" is no more clearer now than it was then. Perhaps it refers to birth from the amniotic fluid in the womb and then death for emergence into new life as a spirit. But the outcome is certain. Paul declares, "Therefore, if anyone is in Christ, the new creation has come. The old has gone, the new is here! All this is from God, who reconciled us to himself through (the sacrifice of) Christ and gave us the ministry of reconciliation" (2 Corinthians 5:17–18).

In contrast, it appears that some people are destined not to accept Christ. Some do not even get the option: "Paul and his companions traveled throughout the region of Phrygia and Galatia, having been kept by the Holy Spirit from preaching the word in the province of Asia. When they came to the border of Mysia, they tried to enter Bithynia, but the Spirit of Jesus would not allow them to" (Acts 16:6–7). However, it appears that Jesus may have changed his mind as later scriptures mention churches in Asia: "This went on for two years, so that all the Jews and Greeks who lived in the province of Asia heard the word of the Lord" (Acts 19:10); "greet my dear friend Epenetus, who was the first convert to Christ in the province of Asia" (Romans 16:5); and "the churches in the province of Asia send you greetings. Aquila and Priscilla greet you warmly in the Lord, and so does the church that meets at their house (1 Corinthians 16:19).

On the other hand, it seems that some disciples were chosen without any choice: "To God's elect, exiles scattered throughout the provinces of Pontus, Galatia, Cappadocia, Asia and Bithynia, who have been chosen according to the foreknowledge of God the Father, through the sanctifying work of the Spirit, to be obedient to Jesus Christ and sprinkled with his blood" (1 Peter 1:1). However, others seem to have a choice: "Ask and it will be given to you; seek and you will find; knock and the door will be opened to you" (Matthew 7:7, Luke 11:9–10). But it seems that some of those who wish to be chosen will be rejected: "Someone asked him, Lord, are only a few people going to be saved? He said to them, Make every effort to enter through the narrow door, because many, I tell you, will try to enter and will not be able to. Once the owner of the house gets up and closes the door, you will stand outside knocking and pleading, Sir, open the door for us. But he will answer, I don't know you or where you come from" (Luke 13:23–25). Are you confused as I am?

Moreover, Jesus taught the disciples in parables, that is, stories with secret meanings that he explained to them in private, but not to others on purpose. When they asked him why he did not provide the same information to everyone, he replied,

> Because the knowledge of the secrets of the kingdom of Heaven has been given to you, but not to them. Whoever has will be given more, and they will have an abundance. Whoever does not have,

even what they have will be taken from them. This is why I speak to them in parables (quoting Isaiah 6:9–10):

Though seeing, they do not see;
though hearing, they do not hear or understand.
In them is fulfilled the prophecy of Isaiah:

You will be ever hearing but never understanding;
you will be ever seeing but never perceiving.
For this people's heart has become calloused;
they hardly hear with their ears,
and they have closed their eyes.
Otherwise they might see with their eyes,
hear with their ears,
<u>understand with their hearts</u>
and turn, and I would heal them.

Another scripture explains the rejection by the Jews who disbelieved in Jesus as inevitable. "They stumble because they disobey the message—which is also what they were destined for" (1 Peter 2:8). However, scripture also implies they had a choice: "Jerusalem, Jerusalem, you who kill the prophets and stone those sent to you, how often I have longed to gather your children together, as a hen gathers her chicks under her wings, and you were not willing" (Matthew 23:37). I am not making this up.

Understanding with the "heart" also was proclaimed by Apostle Paul, so there must be some significance between it and the mind: "I keep asking that the God of our Lord Jesus Christ, the glorious Father, may give you the Spirit of wisdom and revelation, so that you may know him better. I pray that the <u>eyes of your heart</u> may be enlightened in order that you may know the hope to which he has called you, the riches of his glorious inheritance in his holy people, and his incomparably great power for us who believe" (Ephesians 1:17–19) and "the fool <u>says in his heart</u>, there is no God" (Psalm 14:1). The word "heart" is very popular in the Bible, appearing 576 times in the Old Testament and 149 times in the New Testament. The writers seem to distinguish between heart and mind. Heart seems to be a keyword in scripture that invites special study, but that is beyond the scope of this work.

Unfortunately, those who believed did not get off easily. The conditions of Christian discipleship for those who are chosen can be very costly because God apparently wants total commitment, with nothing separating them, except when he doesn't. Jesus told a rich man to sell all he had and donate it to the poor "then come follow me" if he wanted eternal life, but he had too much to lose that he was unwilling to give up. When he walked away, Jesus said, "It is easier for a camel to go through the eye of a needle than for someone who is rich to enter the kingdom of God" (Matthew 19:16–24) and "believers in humble circumstances ought to take pride in their high position. But the rich should take pride in their humiliation—since they will pass away like a wild flower. For the sun rises with scorching heat and withers the plant; its blossom falls, and its beauty is destroyed. In the same way, the rich will fade away even while they go about their business" (James 1:9–11). Perhaps that scripture is the authority by which the Catholic Church requires its priests and nuns to take a vow of poverty and obedience—including celibacy.

Jesus is a tough master. He told a volunteer who wanted to go home and bury his father, "Follow me, and let the dead bury their own dead" (Matthew 8:23); "whoever wants to be my disciple must deny themselves and take up their cross and follow me" (Mark 8:34); and "anyone who loves their father or mother more than me is not worthy of me; anyone who loves their son or daughter more than me is not worthy of me" (Matthew 10:37). He also said, "If anyone comes to me and does not hate father and mother, wife and children, brothers and sisters—yes, even their own life—such a person cannot be my disciple" (Luke 14:26). This scripture seems to contradict the fifth commandment: "Honor your father and mother so your life may be long upon the earth" (Ephesians 6:2, Deuteronomy 5:16). It also conflicts with this scripture: "And he has given us this command: Anyone who loves God must also love their brother and sister" (1 John 4:19–21). Go figure.

Much is said in the New Testament about sowing seeds and reaping harvests in the incipient church of Christ. In parables, Jesus likens his ministry to the sower of seeds in two ways. In one, he uses the analogy of a farmer who finds weeds sown by his enemy growing up with his crop. When asked by his servants if they should pull out the weeds, he tells them to let the weeds grow with the crop and at harvesttime they will be separated and the weeds burned in the trash. Then he explains the crop is his followers and the weeds are the evil ones. In another parable, Jesus explains that the Kingdom of God is like a man who sows the smallest of all seeds, a mustard seed, which grows into the largest tree in the garden. He also tells of a farmer who scatters his seed about so that some falls on pathways where birds eat it up, some falls onto rocks, some falls into thorn bushes that choke it out, and some falls on good soil, referring to someone who hears the Word and understands it. "This is the one who produces a crop, yielding a hundred, sixty or thirty times what was sown" (Matthew 13, Mark 4).

The analogy of seeds and harvest also is used for other purposes in the Bible: "Do not be deceived: God cannot be mocked. A man reaps what he sows. Whoever sows to please their flesh, from the flesh will reap destruction; whoever sows to please the Spirit, from the Spirit will reap eternal life" (Galatians 6:8). The symbol of sowing and reaping also is used to encourage donations for the preaching of the Gospel as in fund-raising. When a poor widow gave all that she had to the temple treasury, Jesus praised her in comparison to rich people who gave from their abundance. (Mark 12:43-44) Poof texting such scriptures encourages poor people to give all they have to a church in hopes they will win the lottery in life. But Jesus declared there will always be poor people, and "blessed are the poor in spirit for theirs is the kingdom of heaven." (Matthew 5:3, 26:11) God must love poor people because "the Lord is the maker of them all." There is no other explanation of how people are selected into rich and poor. (1 Samuel 2:6-7, Proverbs 22:2)

Church fund-raisers invoke scriptures to encourage giving: "Give, and it will be given to you. A good measure, pressed down, shaken together and running over, will be poured into your lap. For with the measure you use, it will be measured to you" (Luke 6:38) and "bring the whole tithe into the storehouse, that there may be food in my house. Test me in this, says the LORD Almighty, and see if I will not throw open the floodgates of heaven and pour out so much blessing that there will not be room enough to store it" (Malachi 3:10).

However, Jesus also told others it would not be so bad: "Come to me, all you who are weary and burdened, and I will give you rest. Take my yoke upon you and learn from me, for I am gentle and humble in heart, and you will find rest for your souls. For my yoke is easy and my burden is light" (Matthew 28:28–29). So you don't have to worry; in fact, you should not worry because he has it all covered: "Can any one of you by worrying add a single hour to your life? And why do you worry about clothes? See how the flowers of the field grow. They do not labor or spin. So, do not worry, saying, What shall we eat? or What shall we drink? or What shall we wear? Therefore, do not worry about tomorrow, for tomorrow will worry about itself. Each day has enough trouble of its own. But seek first his kingdom and his righteousness, and all these things will be given to you as well" (Matthew 6:25–34). That is what it says, but I would not count on it because Apostle Paul wrote, "For even when we were with you, we gave you this rule: The one who is unwilling to work shall not eat." (2 Thessalonians 2:10). Isn't the truth confusing?

Jesus made some very specific promises to his twelve apostles, conditioned upon personal sacrifice: "Truly I tell you, at the renewal of all things, when the Son of Man sits on his glorious throne, you who have followed me will also sit on twelve thrones, judging the twelve tribes of Israel. And everyone who has left houses or brothers or sisters or father or mother or wife or children or fields for my sake will receive a hundred times as much and will inherit eternal life" (Matthew 19:28–30). And he told his disciple one must leave everything, hate his whole family, and take up a cross and follow him (Luke 14:26). These examples show the difficulty in making sense of divergent scriptures, do they not?

It can all get very confusing unless you proof text these scriptures and focus only on the ones you prefer while avoiding the others, that is, cherry-picking. That is what most Christian teachers do, and it must be necessary or it would not be possible. But Jesus did not condone or appreciate such deception. "If anyone causes one of these little ones—those who believe in me—to stumble, it would be better for them to have a large millstone hung around their neck and to be drowned in the depths of the sea" (Matthew 18:6). The problem is that scriptures do not clearly state the truth.

Discussion of the Afterlife

As to what happens after death, the Bible is equally vague and confusing. According to various ideas about the afterlife, the essential aspect of the individual that lives on after death may be some soul or spirit of an individual, which carries with it and may confer personal identity with or without resurrection of a physical body depending upon various interpretations. Jesus declared, "The Spirit gives life, the flesh counts for nothing" (John 6:63). "If there is a natural body, there is also a spiritual body. So it is written: The first man Adam became a living being]; the last Adam, a life-giving spirit" (1 Corinthians 15:43-45). It is described thus in the Old Testament: "The Spirit of God has made me; the breath of the Almighty gives me life" (Job 33:4). "Yet a time is coming and has now come when the true worshipers will worship the Father in the Spirit and in truth, for they are the kind of worshipers the Father seeks. God is spirit, and his worshipers must worship in the Spirit and in truth" (John 3:24–25). Indeed, Pierre Teilhard de Chardin said, "We are not human beings having a spiritual experience; we are spiritual beings having a human experience." Scriptures say a lot about the Holy Spirit—ninety-six times in the New Testament—without ever defining it. Many people call themselves spiritual without being religious, so what does this really mean?

> Perhaps "spirit/soul" refers to energy which, as in the laws of thermodynamics, cannot be either created nor destroyed. Thus, as with God, it may have no beginning or ending that we can understand. The concept of energy was not developed until the nineteenth

century, so the writers of the Bible knew nothing about it. Energy is depicted in several different forms, one of which may be called "life." "The body without spirit/energy is dead" (James 2:26). Thus, I have a body, but I am not my body. UK biologist Rupert Sheldrake has proposed existence of undetectable morphic energy fields and telepathic communications. Strong emotions can feel contagious because they may create strong fields, such as the mood at funerals compared to the mood at football games.

Such fields could be created by vibrations of the atoms making up the elements in sentient bodies. They may be detected with Kirlian photography that captures the light, called aura, around living bodies. This theory helps explain why some people are attracted and some are repelled and how some people seem to experience feelings beyond the senses, what might be called premonitions—not unlike electromagnetism. Also, it could explain the affection between people and their pets. Some studies have shown critical-care patients recover quicker with less stress if they are prayed for, even when they don't know it, invoking speculations about possible resonant energy fields. This theory could explain the "self" that cannot know itself, the "I am that I am." And it could help to explain what C. G. Jung described as intuition, "the ability to see around corners." The US Defense Advanced Research Projects Agency has conducted experiments showing the possibility of energetic communications between minds at long distances. For more details on morphic energy, visit www.sheldrake.org.

Belief in a conscious afterlife is in contrast to oblivion after death, a state of sleep until the day of resurrection when all who are chosen will be risen to live with the Lord. When Jesus received news of his death, he said, "Our friend Lazarus has fallen asleep; but I am going there to wake him up. His disciples replied, Lord, if he sleeps, he will get better. Jesus had been speaking of his death, but his disciples thought he meant natural sleep" (John 11:11–12). "We will not all sleep, but we will all be changed in a flash, in the twinkling of an eye, at the last trumpet. For the trumpet will sound, the dead will be raised imperishable, and we will be changed" (1 Corinthians 15:50–

52). It appears this change will be a transformation from the physical to the spiritual since the body returns to the earth. Jesus declared that in heaven there will no marriage or giving in marriage, and we will be like angels—whatever they are (Matthew 22:30, Mark 12:25, Luke 20:34–36). I understand that Mormons believe families can be "sealed" for all eternity, seemingly ignoring this scripture. As for marriage on earth, the Apostle Paul votes against it so everyone can devote their full attention to preparation for the imminent return of Christ as he does, except for those who cannot contain their passions because "it is better to marry than to burn" (1 Corinthians 7).

There also is an inference in reincarnation, that is, the soul returns to life many times throughout history to learn and develop until it achieves the ultimate perfection or nirvana, after which no more lives are necessary. When Jesus asked the disciples who people thought he was, they replied, "Some say John the Baptist; others say Elijah; and still others, Jeremiah or one of the prophets" Matthew 16:14). "But about the resurrection of the dead—have you not read what God said to you, I am the God of Abraham, the God of Isaac, and the God of Jacob? He is not the God of the dead but of the living. When the crowds heard this, they were astonished at his teaching" (Matthew 22:31–33). Jesus took Peter, James, and John to a high mountain where Moses and Elijah also appeared and talked with Jesus. As they were coming down the mountain, the disciples asked Jesus, "Why then do the teachers of the law say that Elijah must come first? Jesus replied, To be sure, Elijah comes and will restore all things. But I tell you, Elijah has already come, and they did not recognize him, but have done to him everything they wished. In the same way the Son of Man is going to suffer at their hands. Then the disciples understood that he was talking to them about John the Baptist" (Matthew 17:1–13). The Old Testament prophesied Elijah himself, not someone like him or someone in the same ministry as him, but Elijah himself would return before the advent of the Messiah (Malachi 4:5).

Based upon these scriptures, only one of the following can be true: reincarnation is real, or Jesus was not the Messiah, or Old Testament prophecies are not reliable. However, the Bible also says we have only one life to live and one death and after that the judgment (Hebrews 9:27). Therefore, it is said that reincarnation was expelled from Christian dogma by edict of Roman emperor Justinian the Great in 553 CE. The Kabbalah branch of Judaism still includes reincarnation in its dogma. You see, the problem with proof texting the scriptures is one cannot tell what is a comment meant specifically for that time and place only and what is a generality meant for all times and places. And this dilemma must be necessary, or it would be different.

The Jewish traditions, which do not conceive of the afterlife as a place of punishment or reward, merely describe hell as an abode of the dead, the grave, a neutral place located under the surface of earth referred to as Sheol and Hades (not to be confused with the Greek Hades, god of the underworld.) While the Old Testament appears to describe Sheol as the permanent place of the dead, in the Second Temple period (roughly 500 BCE–70 CE), a more diverse set of ideas developed. In some scriptures, Sheol is considered to be the home of both the righteous and the wicked, separated into respective compartments; in others, it was considered a place of punishment, meant for the wicked dead alone, and is equated with Gehenna in the Talmud. When the Hebrew scriptures were translated into Greek in ancient Alexandria around 200 BCE, the word "Hades" (the Greek underworld) was substituted for Sheol. This is reflected in the New Testament where Hades is both the underworld of the dead and the personification of the evil it represents, possibly the Greek god Hades. The Catholic Church created a place of temporary abode for upgrading of souls not quite good enough to enter heaven they call Purgatory (*Wikipedia*).

There is a "Discourse to the Greeks Concerning Hades" believed to be the work of Hippolytus of Rome. Hippolytus (AD 170–235) was one of the most important third-century theologians in the Christian Church in Rome, where he was probably born. It was first published in a translation of the first-century historian, Josephus, by English theologian, William Whiston (1667–1752). It appears in many present-day English editions of Josephus's work without noting its erroneous attribution. The author assures the Greeks he is addressing that God will resurrect the dead, raising again their present bodies and not transmigrating their souls to heavenly bodies. He insists that God is able to do this, likening the dead body both to sown seed and to material cast into "a potter's furnace, in order to be formed again." The author says that when clothed with their pure resurrected bodies, the just will no longer be subject to disease or misery. The unjust, in contrast, will receive their bodies unchanged, including their original diseases. All (just and unjust) will be brought before Jesus Christ who will come to judge both living and dead. Christ will exercise the righteous judgment of the Father toward all men, with everlasting punishment for the wicked and eternal bliss for the righteous. The author exhorts his audience to believe in God in order to participate in the reward of the just. As with so many theologians to follow, Hippolytus fails to reference any scriptures to support his exegesis.

Jesus declared, "Truly I tell you, this generation will certainly not pass away until all these things have happened. Heaven and earth will pass away, but my words will never pass away" (Matthew 24:34–35). It turns out that Jesus was wrong on the timing, if not the prophecy. Hippolytus did not subscribe to the belief that the Second Coming of Christ was imminent, which it wasn't. He was the first, but not the last, to set a specific date for the Second Advent through calculation—500CE—which was 260 years after his time. He assumed that since God made all things in six days, and these days symbolize a thousand years each, in six thousand years from the creation, the end will come. He apparently based his calculation on the Septuagint—the oldest issue of the Old Testament—which had the world beginning about 5500 BCE. Other forecasters have predicted the end of the world from time to time, but all of them have been wrong up to now. One thing seems to be certain, and that is uncertainty. "When you hear of wars and rumors of wars (or uprisings,) do not be alarmed (or afraid.) Such things must happen, but the end is still to come (or will not come right away)" (Mark 13:7, Luke 21:9). In fact, if there is only one word that defines life on earth, it might be violence. Indeed, the history of humankind is driven more by war than by peace. Perhaps we should thank God for providing competitive sports and violent video games to absorb the energy that might otherwise be applied to shedding real blood even more. The façade of civilization is very thin.

Be that as it may, Jesus tried to reassure his disciples of his plan for their future: "Do not let your hearts be troubled. You believe in God; believe also in me. My Father's house has many rooms; if that were not so, would I have told you that I am going there to prepare a place for you? And if I go and prepare a place for you, I will come back and take you to be with me so that you also may be where I am" (John 14:1–3) Although this scripture is directed to the disciples present at that time and place without reference to any others, often it is used for proof texting by claiming it applies to all believers everywhere at all times.

However, for the others who reject him, the outcome is very unpleasant. "The Son of Man will send out his angels and they will weed out of his kingdom everything that causes sin and all who do evil. They will throw them into the blazing furnace, where there will be weeping and gnashing of teeth. Then the righteous will shine like the sun in the kingdom of their Father. Whoever has ears, let them hear" (Matthew 13:40-43). The timing of these terminal events is known only to God, and even Jesus was not given the specifics. Angels (a.k.a. cherubim and seraphim) are mentioned in the New International Version 14 times in the Old Testament and 84 times in the New Testament—23 of them in Revelation. In the New American Standard Bible, angels appear 103 times in the Old Testament and 93 times in the New Testament. Whatever we may be, the Bible says humans are created just a little lower than angels (Hebrews 2:7). From the stupid and insane behavior of many people, that does not say much about angels. They would make an interesting study, but for another time. For a detailed discussion, visit www. https://bible.org/article/angelology-doctrine-angels.

Thus, we see again the Bible presents confusing and dialectically opposed scriptures about the basic dogma of Christianity. Only by proof texting can it be said, "All scripture is given by inspiration of God, and is profitable for doctrine, for reproof, for correction, for instruction in righteousness" (2 Timothy 3:16) The New Testament gospels were not yet available, so Dr. Robert M. Price thinks Paul was referring to other writings that were omitted from scriptures.

Taken as a whole, Bible scriptures are more confusing than comforting, in my opinion.

The ascension of Jesus back into heaven after his resurrection marked the end of his work on earth for this time. On the cross he declared, "It is finished." The four Gospels end in four different ways. Each one must have its purpose, or it would be different. So it is worthwhile to read each of them as written:

Matthew 28:16–20

> Then the eleven disciples went to Galilee, to the mountain where Jesus had told them to go. When they saw him, they worshiped him; but some doubted. Then Jesus came to them and said, "All authority in Heaven and on earth has been given to me. Therefore, go and make disciples of all nations, baptizing them in the name of the Father and of the Son and of the Holy Spirit, and teaching them to obey everything I have commanded you. And surely, I am with you always, to the very end of the age." As it was then, today missionaries can be imprisoned for taking the gospel to some nations if they threaten established powers. Plus, they must live in the local communities, so it must be a very special calling.
>
> Trinitarians use such scriptures as evidence that God, Son, and Holy Spirit are three in one, but it is a flimsy argument not supported by other scriptures as presented above. The formal definition of the Trinity doctrine was incorporated in the Nicene Creed at the Council of Nicaea that was organized by Emperor Theodosius in 381 CE, after it was argued in 325 CE and 360 CE at the Councils of Ephesus and Constantinople

respectively. The Trinity had to be inferred because it is not explicitly defined in any scriptures. Possibly, the closest scripture is, "For there are three that testify: the Spirit, the water and the blood; and the three are in agreement" (1 John 5:7–8). The Nicene Creed has been edited from time to time, but it is accepted by most Christian churches as their basic dogma. It appears to be the least that one must believe to be a Christian. A modern translation is presented in appendix C.

Mark 16:15–20

He said to them, "Go into all the world and preach the gospel to all creation. Whoever believes and is baptized will be saved, but whoever does not believe will be condemned. And these signs will accompany those who believe: In my name they will drive out demons; they will speak in new tongues; they will pick up snakes with their hands; and when they drink deadly poison, it will not hurt them at all; they will place their hands on sick people, and they will get well. After the Lord Jesus had spoken to them, he was taken up into Heaven and he sat at the right hand of God. Then the disciples went out and preached everywhere, and the Lord worked with them and confirmed his word by the signs that accompanied it."

Some literal interpreters have not fared well playing with snakes and poisons. In fact, none of the promised signs are evident in most Christian churches, except for the Pentecostals who observe speaking in tongues and practice faith healing and a very few who handle snakes in worship services. None of them are tempted to ingest lethal poisons.

Luke 24: 50–53

> When he had led them out to the vicinity of Bethany, he lifted up his hands and blessed them. While he was blessing them, he left them and was taken up into Heaven. Then they worshiped him and returned to Jerusalem with great joy. And they stayed continually at the temple, praising God. (Writers of the Bible seem to think heaven was above the visible sky while hell was below the depths of the earth.)

John 21:18–25

> Jesus said, "Feed my sheep. Very truly I tell you, when you were younger you dressed yourself and went where you wanted; but when you are old you will stretch out your hands, and someone else will dress you and lead you where you do not want to go. Jesus said this to indicate the kind of death by which Peter would glorify God. Then he said to him, "Follow me!" Peter turned and saw that the disciple whom Jesus loved was following them. This was the one who had leaned back against Jesus at the supper and had said, "Lord, who is going to betray you?" When Peter saw him, he asked, "Lord, what about him?" Jesus answered, "If I want him to remain alive until I return, what is that to you? You must follow me." Because of this, the rumor spread among the believers that this disciple would not die. But Jesus did not say that he would not die; he only

said, "If I want him to remain alive until I return, what is that to you?

This is the disciple who testifies to these things and who wrote them down. We know that his testimony is true. Jesus did many other things as well. If every one of them were written down, I suppose, that even the whole world would not have room for the books that would be written."

The Incipient Church of Christ

The Bible says little about the organization, liturgy, and leadership of the apostolic churches. That would have to be done by the writers who followed the generation of the apostles, Athanasius, Augustine, Benedict, Clement, Cyrian, Cyril, Eusebius, Ignatius, Irenaeus, Origen, Tertullian, Polycarp, and others. One would need to read many of these writers to develop an understanding of the "Fathers of the Church" in the first four centuries. The church fathers included popes, attorneys, orators, teachers, activists, and some contemplatives who were hermits. Apparently, there was much wrangling and disputations among the early church writers for and against many different interpretations of scriptures. Most early Christians were illiterate, and what is now the New Testament was spread by oral instruction, which included tradition, homilies, and liturgy. The early church fathers not only had to deal with heresy and various interpretations, but they had to cope with severe persecution, torture, and martyrdom (*Aquiline, The Fathers of the Church*, 2006).

Dr. Robert M. Price attempted to chronicle fifty-four unofficial books that predated the final canon, which helps to explain the many competing approaches to Christian theology prior to adoption of the Nicene Creed in 381 CE. He claims that much, if not most, of the New Testament came from older, even pagan sources that had been known for centuries before, so it is not original. Dr. Price claims that early Christianity was a real jumble of different faiths and viewpoints by various leaders competing for authority that only congealed into something vaguely resembling what we have today sometime in the third century. Christians may not like to accept that notion, but Price produces abundant scholarly evidence. Trying to sort it all out and arrive at an objective history about what really happened in the first three centuries after Christ is all but impossible (*The Pre-Nicene New Testament*, 2006). By the end of the fourth century, St. Jerome could compile short biographies of 135 writers in the incipient church from Apostle Peter down to himself. Emperor Theodosius called the Council of Nicaea in 381 CE to sort out the variations and consolidate the beliefs of the church in the Nicene Creed. Thereafter, he proclaimed Christianity as the official church of Rome, not so much for religious unity, but rather for political stability. Of course, this historical uncertainty does not matter to the faithful who believe the Bible is the "Word of God" because it says so—132 times.

The Roman emperors who ordered persecutions included Nero (54–68), Domitian (81–96), Trajan (98-117), Antoninus Pius (138–161), Marcus Aurelius (161–180), and Diocletian (284–305). Constantine (305–337) was the first emperor to stop the persecution of Christians and to legalize Christianity, along with all other religions and cults in the Roman Empire. In February 313 CE, he met with Licinius (who would be his opponent in a civil war of 324 CE) in Milan and developed the Edict of Milan, which stated that Christians should be allowed to follow their faith without oppression. The document had special benefits for Christians, legalizing their religion and granting them restoration for all property seized during Diocletian's persecution. Constantine also decreed that Sunday would be a day of rest for all citizens. He supported the Church financially, built basilicas, granted privileges to clergy (such as exemption from certain taxes), promoted Christians to high office, and returned property confiscated during the long period of persecution. His most famous building projects include the Church of the Holy Sepulchre and Old Saint Peter's Basilica. It is said that Constantine accepted Christ on his deathbed and was baptized by Eusebius (*Wikipedia*).

Thousands of more writers contributed over the centuries to what has become the dogma of modern churches, hence the wide range of interpretations even among neighboring churches in the same denominations and among members in the same congregation. The Roman Catholic Church attempts to solve this diversity by demanding obedience to the infallible authority of the pope sitting on his throne in the Vatican—which was declared by Pius IX in 1870. His acceptance as the ultimate voice of God and primal head of the Roman Catholic Church reminds of another primal authority in recent history. Here is a quote provided by the late cosmic scientist Carl Sagan from a speech on June 30, 1934, by Nazi Party leader Rudolf Hess: "One man remains beyond all criticism, and that is the Fuhrer. This is because everyone senses and knows he is always right, and he will always be right. The National Socialism of all of us is anchored in uncritical loyalty, in surrender to the Fuhrer." To which Adolf Hitler declared, "What good fortune for those in power that (some) people do not think" (*Billions and Billions*, 1998, 190).

Hitler had little regard for writers whom he called "fops of the pen" who for leadership are "neither born nor chosen...every great movement on this earth owes its growth to orators and not to great writers." He actually had contempt for the German masses "who are slow moving and always require a certain time before they are ready to notice anything and then only after ideas are repeated thousands of times will the masses remember them" (*Mein Kampf*, 1925). Perhaps this is why the Catholic mass is so highly structured and celebrated so often and why President Trump keeps repeating his slogan, "Make America Great Again."

Hitler's oratorical skill caused the death of fifty-five million people in WWII. In contrast, the oratorical skill of the late evangelist Billy Graham brought the redemption of many people, another example of necessary opposites and God's will in action. It seems that people—created by God—have the abilities both to think and to be duped, whether by oratorical politicians or by preachers.

Proof texting scripture may not be lying, but it certainly is not telling the full truth to those who can be duped. As President Donald J. Trump apparently learned, if you repeat a lie often enough, during stressful times, some people will believe it is true. He is the first president to use social media effectively as his primary means of communication. His grandiose faux omnipotence seems to be appealing to his helpless followers—like the apparent authority of Jesus during Jewish oppression by the Romans or the authority Jews bestowed upon Simon Bar Kokhba to lead the final revolution in 135 CE. Great people talk about ideas, average people talk about things, and little people talk about other people. For such people, lies will "trump" the truth—pun intended. Reports indicate 80 percent of evangelicals voted for Trump in spite of his alleged immorality, which seems at odds with the Gospel of Jesus and the Kingdom of God as he taught in the parables. One may only say of the success of Hitler, Trump, and the pope, including Jesus, it must be God's will or it would be different. How else can one explain such things? Indeed, Jesus referred to his followers as "sheep" twenty-nine times in the four Gospels. Sheep follow the first one in line regardless of where it leads them. Wake up, sheeple! Jesus said, "If the blind lead the blind, both will fall into a pit" (Matthew 15:14). Sheeple often say "God is in control" without pondering what that really means. But whatever happens, it must be the will of God, or it would be different. Get it?

Actually, it was Jesus himself who began telling his story first to his twelve apostles and then to various groups in the villages within walking distance of the Sea of Galilee, and later, Jerusalem. One may only wonder where he got his education because the Bible does not explain the years of his youth except to describe him discussing scripture with the temple priests at the age of twelve. (Luke 2:41-45)

Jesus's method of teaching recorded in the Gospels involved parables, metaphor, allegory, proverbs, and a small number of original sermons. The most impressive and demanding is the one commonly called "The Sermon on the Mount" found in Matthew chapters 5–7, which established Jesus as "one having authority." Authority is in the mind of the reader, and minds obviously can be controlled by promises for good or evil. It is duplicated with variations as the "Sermon on the Plain" in Luke 6:20–22. You won't find it preached often in churches because it turned social standards upside down, then as now. His sermon contains a list of eight "beatitudes" that assign blessings to the poor suffering souls among humankind. Jesus did not remove the suffering, but merely blessed those who suffer. He also admonished the rich, the laughing, the well fed, and those who are honored in this life by declaring, "Woe to you." If everyone had heaven on earth there would be no need to hope for anything better hereafter, but we don't, and we do.

The Bible says Jesus selected twelve men from various occupations to be his special followers who would take his message to the Jews and become "fishers of men." The Bible does not say how many recruits rejected his offer. He taught them privately in the form of parables the secrets of the Kingdom of God. Peter, John, and James are given primary roles in the scriptures, but the others fade into history. In addition, he appointed a group to go ahead as advance evangelists to make way for him in the cities on his planned itinerary: "The Lord appointed seventy-two others and sent them two by two ahead of him to every town and place where he was about to go. He told them the harvest is plentiful, but the workers are few. Ask the Lord of the harvest, therefore, to send out workers into his harvest field. Go! I am sending you out like lambs among wolves. Do not take a purse or bag or sandals; and do not greet anyone on the road… Whoever listens to you listens to me; whoever rejects you rejects me; but whoever rejects me rejects him who sent me… The seventy-two returned with joy and said, Lord, even the demons submit to us in your name" (Luke 10:1–4, 17). So by the time of his departure from earth about three years later, there likely were some established converts among the Jews of Galilee, however small or large a number we cannot know.

The coming of the church of Christ after his departure rests on two scriptures (Matthew 16:13–20): "When Jesus came to the region of Caesarea Philippi, he asked his disciples, Who do people say the Son of Man is? They replied, Some say John the Baptist; others say Elijah; and still others, Jeremiah or one of the prophets. (Elsewhere Jesus declared, "Before Elijah was, I am.") But what about you? he asked. Who do you say I am? Simon Peter answered, You are the Messiah, the Son of the living God. Jesus replied, blessed are you, Simon son of Jonah, for this was not revealed to you by flesh and blood, but by my Father in Heaven. And I tell you that you are Peter, and on this rock I will build my church, and the gates of Hades will not overcome it. I will give you the keys of the kingdom of Heaven;

whatever you bind on earth will be bound in Heaven, and whatever you loose on earth will be loosed in Heaven. Then he ordered his disciples not to tell anyone that he was the Messiah" (Matthew 28:16–20).

After the resurrection: "Then the eleven disciples (*absent Judas the betrayer*) went to Galilee, to the mountain where Jesus had told them to go. When they saw him, they worshiped him; but some doubted. Then Jesus came to them and said, All authority in Heaven and on earth has been given to me. Therefore, go and make disciples of all nations, baptizing them in the name of the Father and of the Son and of the Holy Spirit, and teaching them to obey everything I have commanded you. And, surely, I am with you always, to the very end of the age." (The Bible does not contain a succinct list of the commandments of Jesus, so after searching the Internet, I found a list and posted them in appendix A.*)*

Jesus provided few, if any, instructions about organizing and conducting affairs of his church. Before there was a church, the Bible contains this scripture: "If your brother or sister sins, go and point out their fault, just between the two of you. If they listen to you, you have won them over. But if they will not listen, take one or two others along, so that every matter may be established by the testimony of two or three witnesses. If they still refuse to listen, tell it to the church; and if they refuse to listen even to the church, treat them as you would a pagan or a tax collector" (Matthew 18:15–18). This instruction seems to be at odds with other scriptures describing the relationship between tax collectors and Jesus, as follows:

> While Jesus was having dinner at Matthew's house (notice this third-person account is in the book of Matthew, which challenges its authorship), many tax collectors and sinners came and ate with him and his disciples. When the Pharisees saw this, they asked his disciples, "Why does your teacher eat with tax collectors and sinners? On hearing this, Jesus said, It is not the healthy who need a doctor, but the sick. But go and learn what this

means: I desire mercy, not sacrifice. For I have not come to call the righteous, but sinners." (Matthew 9:10–12)

For John the Baptist came neither eating bread nor drinking wine, and you say, He has a demon. The Son of Man came eating and drinking, and you say, Here is a glutton and a drunkard, a friend of tax collectors and sinners. But wisdom is proved right by all her children. (John 7:33–35)

So did Jesus condemn tax collectors or favor them?

The first church described in Jerusalem apparently was organized by Apostle Peter, thereafter to be proclaimed the first pope by the Catholic Church. Their mutual devotion was so complete that members of the first congregation sold all their possessions and pooled their wealth to live in a communal setting governed by the apostles who distributed to each according to their needs.

Jesus had ordered, "Do not store up for yourselves treasures on earth, where moths and vermin destroy, and where thieves break in and steal. But store up for yourselves treasures in heaven, where moths and vermin do not destroy, and where thieves do not break in and steal. For where your treasure is, there your heart will be also" (Matthew 6:17–21). Failure to conform and withholding of personal wealth from communal needs was met with sudden death as was demonstrated by the married couple, Ananias and Sapphira, who failed to give all they had. After they both were struck dead, "Great fear seized the whole church and all who heard about these events" (Acts 5:1–11). Killing anyone who disobeys and withholds their wealth surely is an effective way to enforce obedience and compile money for church treasuries. From time to time, a new self-proclaimed prophet has attempted to replicate conditions of absolute loyalty in a cult like the first church, but they have imploded and disappeared with much suffering and death of the members. Examples in recent times include the Jonestown massacre, the Branch Davidians fire, and the Heaven's Gate mass suicide.

By the way, healing the sick seems to be related to "laying on hands," which is mentioned twenty-five times in the New Testament. This practice now is used as both a symbolic and formal method of invoking the Holy Spirit primarily during baptisms and confirmations; healing services; blessings; and ordination of priests, ministers, elders, deacons, and other church officers, along with a variety of other church sacraments and holy ceremonies. It also is part of alternative medicine, which is related to the placebo effect by modern science—the belief in efficacy of a sugar pill if you trust the provider—similar to faith in God. However, Jesus did tell his disciples they could have whatever they prayed for if they believed it (Matthew 21:22; Matthew 9:22, 29, 15:28).

> Hands-on healing was developed in Japan in 1922 by Mikau Usui, which he called Reiki therapy. The Nurse Healers Association adopted it in 1979 as authorized practice, which has morphed into the Therapeutic Touch International Association. It claims, "Therapeutic Touch® is a holistic, evidence-based therapy that incorporates the intentional and compassionate use of universal energy to promote balance and well-being. It is based on the idea that human beings are energy (undetectable so far) in the form of a field. When you are healthy, that energy is freely flowing and balanced. In contrast, disease is a condition of energy imbalance or disorder which can be corrected with compassionate touch. It is being taught in more than 100 countries." Sufficient public health interest maintains research in this and other alternative medicine by the National Center for Complementary and Integrative Health at the US National Institutes of Health. For details, visit www.nccih.nih.gov and www.theurapeutictouch.org.

During the missionary journeys by Apostle Paul, he apparently earned his living as a tent maker and expected believers to earn their own living (Acts 18:2–4, 1 Corinthians 4:11–13): "Yet we urge you, brothers and sisters to make it your ambition to lead a quiet life: You should mind your own business and work with your hands, just as we told you, so that your daily life may win the respect of outsiders and so that you will not be dependent on anybody" (1 Thessalonians 4:10–11); "for even when we were with you, we gave you this rule: 'The one who is unwilling to work shall not eat'" (2 Thessalonians 3:10). However, elsewhere he authorized workers in the Gospel to be justly compensated, even though he himself would serve the Lord voluntarily without pay so no one could say he was just doing it for the money (1 Corinthians 9:15–19). "Unlike so many, we do not peddle the word of God for profit" (2 Corinthians 2:17). Moreover, Jesus taught his disciples to "be in the world but not of the world" just as he was (John 17:14–16).

But wait, scripture also says in the voice of Paul, "This is my defense to those who sit in judgment on me. Don't we have the right to food and drink? Don't we have the right to take a believing wife along with us, as do the other apostles and the Lord's brothers and Cephas? Or is it only I and Barnabas who lack the right to not work for a living? If we have sown spiritual seed among you, is it too much if we reap a material harvest from you?" (1 Corinthians 9:3–6, 11). Is this the same man who said he was single and organized churches without pay in the verses above? Notice the unique mention of "the Lord's brothers." So what are you going to believe?

Ministry has become a full-time profession and, for some, a pathway to fame and riches. However, some of the most successful pastors of megachurches and televangelists are not seminary graduates. What they seem to have in common is effective oratory and the ability to proof-text scriptures. They really are good at what they do—all in God's will, of course. Church members actually contribute little to nothing to the ministry of Jesus now, apart from depositing their tithes and offerings during their once-a-week attendance.

Nevertheless, Jesus told his disciples: "You are the light of the world. A town built on a hill cannot be hidden. Neither do people light a lamp and put it under a bowl. Instead they put it on its stand, and it gives light to everyone in the house. In the same way, let your light shine before others, that they may see your good deeds and glorify your Father in heaven" (Matthew 5:14–16). But wait, he also told them to give to the needy, to pray, and to fast in secret so the left hand will not know what the right hand is doing so you will not be obvious, except to the Father who will reward you: "Be careful not to practice your righteousness in front of others to be seen by them. If you do, you will have no reward from your Father in heaven. So, when you give to the needy, do not announce it with trumpets, as the hypocrites do in the synagogues and on the streets, to be honored by others. Truly I tell you, they have received their reward in full" (Matthew 6:1–8, 18). Do these two scriptures contradict or support each other? It seems like the writer of chapter 5 was not the same person who wrote chapter 6. One apologist wrote, "There is a significant difference in being seen doing good works and in doing good works to be seen. Considering the importance of directing attention to God's goodness when giving alms, and the competing desire to impress others with one's righteousness, it makes sense that Matthew 6:1-4 strongly prohibits shining a spotlight on oneself." This is a good example of how proof texting scriptures can produce different interpretations, which must be the way God wants it or it would be different.

The years following the departure of Jesus until the death of the last of the twelve apostles are called the Apostolic Age. The apostolic period produced the books of the New Testament attributed to some of the direct followers of Jesus and is traditionally associated with the apostles and apostolic times. Apparently, according to Dr. Robert M. Price, many other writings during those years did not survive the selection process that resulted in the canon, that is, the official books of the New Testament. The Church of Christ came fully into being on the day of Pentecost when, according to the book of Acts, many disciples received the Holy Spirit and emerged from hiding after the death and resurrection of Jesus to preach and spread his message with new vigor and confidence. The purpose of local churches is given thus: "To equip the saints for the work of ministry, for building up the body of Christ, until all of us come to the unity of the faith and of the knowledge of the Son of God, to maturity, to the measure of the full stature of Christ" (Ephesians 4:12–13).

A contentious issue obtains from the departing words of Jesus to his disciples: "And these signs will accompany those who believe: In my name they will drive out demons; they will speak in new tongues" (Mark 16:17) and "you will receive power when the Holy Spirit comes on you; and you will be my witnesses in Jerusalem, and in all Judea and Samaria, and to the ends of the earth" (Acts 1:8). Scholars claim this scripture was fulfilled at the day of Pentecost that occurred fifty days after the ascension of Jesus in Jerusalem among a crowd of disciples who were gathered there in one room.

> They saw what seemed to be tongues of fire that separated and came to rest on each of them. All of them were filled with the Holy Spirit and began to speak in other tongues as the Spirit enabled them. Now there were staying in Jerusalem God-fearing Jews from every nation under Heaven. When they heard this sound, a crowd came together in bewilderment, because each one heard their own language being spoken. Utterly amazed, they asked: Aren't all these who are speaking Galileans? Then how is it that each of us hears them in our native language? Parthians, Medes and Elamites; residents of Mesopotamia, Judea and Cappadocia, Pontus and Asia, Phrygia and Pamphylia, Egypt and the parts of Libya near Cyrene; visitors from Rome (both Jews and converts to Judaism); Cretans and Arabs—we hear them declaring the wonders of God in our own tongues! Amazed and perplexed, they asked one another, "What does this mean?" Peter stood up and addressed the crowd. "These people are not drunk, as you suppose. It's only nine in the morning! No, this is what was spoken by the prophet Joel: In the last days, God says, I will pour out my Spirit on all people" (Acts 2:1–17).

This event also fulfilled the promise of Jesus to send a "comforter" after his departure to complete the Trinity of Father, Son, and Holy Ghost as three-in-one, which would empower the church to withstand its inevitable persecution and to be its advocate in the world (John 14:16). Three (3) seems to be a very significant number because it occurs 297 times in the Old Testament and 84 times in the New Testament (NIV). Possibly its most significance is the death of Jesus at 3:00 PM and his resurrection after three days. Thereafter, it is reported, "When Paul placed his hands on them, the Holy Spirit came on them, and they spoke in tongues and prophesied" (Acts 19:16). From these scriptures, some churches have concluded that speaking in tongues (called glossolalia) is a prerequisite to "baptism in the Holy Spirit" that Jesus declared is necessary to be "born again," which is necessary to be saved (John 3:5–7).

Paul wrote about tongues twelve times in 1 Corinthians 12–15, giving what seems to be both support and rejection as a gift of the spirit, but with strings attached:

> To another faith by the same Spirit, to another gifts of healing by that one Spirit, to another miraculous powers, to another prophecy, to another distinguishing between spirits, to another speaking in different kinds of tongues (a.k.a. languages) and to still another the interpretation of tongues. All these are the work of one and the same Spirit, and he distributes them to each one, just as he determines… I thank God that I speak in tongues more than all of you. But in the church, I would rather speak five intelligible words to instruct others than ten thousand words in a tongue… So if the whole church comes together and everyone speaks in tongues, and inquirers or unbelievers come in, will they not say that you are out of your mind? (1 Corinthians 12:9–17, 14:18–23)

> If anyone speaks in a tongue, two—or at the most three—should speak, one at a time, and someone must interpret. (1 Corinthians 14:27)

This subject is not mentioned anywhere else in the New Testament, and it disappeared from discussions by the later writers who were taught by the apostles and, except for some scattered mentions in churches during the latter centuries, was dormant thereafter. Nevertheless, it became a contentious topic during a revival in the early twentieth century beginning in Southern California and expanded with the charismatic movement in the 1960s among Pentecostal churches. Modern research using brain scans shows that glossolalia does not activate the speech center of the brain. So if it is evidence of "baptism in the spirit" or not remains a mystery. Whether it is from God or Satan, it must be necessary for those who do it, or it would be different.

Scholars say the original church communities were founded by apostles and numerous other Christians, soldiers, merchants, and preachers in northern Africa, Asia Minor, Arabia, Greece, and other places. Saul of Tarsus, a.k.a. Paul, who was a persecutor of Christians, was called by Jesus himself (in spirit, of course) to bring Christianity to new parts of the Greek world, so it says in the book of Acts (Acts 13:9). The first Christian communities outside of Jerusalem appeared in Antioch, Ephesus, Corinth, and the political center of Rome. They were first called Christians at Antioch. Christianity spread very quickly throughout Asia Minor with more than forty churches established by 100 CE. By the end of the first century, Christianity had already spread to Rome and to various cities in Greece, Asia Minor, and Syria. Modern archaeology has unearthed some of the places buried under 20–30 feet of soil, tending to validate the historicity of these reports.

The Gospel According to Paul

What we can know about these original first-century churches is given by content and inference of letters from the Apostle Paul; the Apostle John; James, the brother of Jesus; Apostle Peter, the rock and foundation of the church; and whoever wrote the Acts of the Apostles and the book of Hebrews. When Paul, a.k.a. Saul of Tarsus, born a Jewish Pharisee but also a Roman citizen, was converted in a flash of light on his trek to Damascus to raid and arrest Christians under authority of the temple priests, the Lord said, "This man is my chosen instrument to proclaim my name to the Gentiles and their kings and to the people of Israel. I will show him how much he must suffer for my name" (Acts 9:15). Apparently, the writer was given this information sometime after the departure of Jesus and the defection of almost all the original twelve. If Paul was not called to suffer, the Bible and history of Christianity would be much different. It just does not pay to be the Lord's advocate. In addition to persecutions, imprisonment, and floggings, Paul apparently suffered some chronic disability: "I was given a thorn in my flesh, a messenger of Satan, to torment me. Three times I pleaded with the Lord to take it away from me. But he said to me, My grace is sufficient for you, for my power is made perfect in weakness. Therefore, I will boast all the more gladly about my weaknesses, so that Christ's power may rest on me. That is why, for Christ's sake, I delight in weaknesses, in insults, in hardships, in persecutions, in difficulties. For when I am weak, then I am strong" (2 Corinthians 12:7–10). Nevertheless, he would later write, "I have learned to be content in whatever situation I am in. I know how to be humble, and I know how to prosper. In each and every situation, I have learned the secret of being full and of going hungry, of having too much and of having too little" (Philippians 4:11–12). Pity that he did not explain his little secret so we could make use of it.

> In Buddhism, contentment is taught as the antidote to desire/discontent/craving, which is the cause of all suffering. The seventh rule of right living requires letting go of the desire for things to be different. Since everything we cling to in life is impermanent, and its loss causes suffering, letting go of all attachment is the solution. If you can let go a little, you experience a little peace, and if you let go more you gain more peace. Complete detachment from all attachments eliminates suffering, including attachment to our own bodies at pending death. This process requires invoking the command and control center of the brain to recognize and retrain behavior to feel

> good inside no matter what happens outside. After all, is this not the goal of all religions? The irony in Buddhism is to convert discontent/desire into contentment, first one must become discontented with suffering. However, American capitalism is driven by discontent because it creates progress. We remain in bondage to desire because we see it as our means to happiness. Much of our lifestyle was driven by discontent in the past, and the future is being driven by desire in the present. But, there are contented indigenous human tribes on earth still living as hunter-gatherers who have not changed in centuries. Suffering is a problem only if you wish things were different. All in God's will of course. (Wikipedia)

There are debates among scholars as to whether Paul understood himself as commissioned to take the Gospel to the Gentiles at the moment of his conversion. After all, he was a Jew first and a Christian later. "If someone else thinks they have reasons to put confidence in the flesh, I have more: circumcised on the eighth day, of the people of Israel, of the tribe of Benjamin, a Hebrew of Hebrews; in regard to the law, a Pharisee; as for zeal, persecuting the church; as for righteousness based on the law, faultless" (Philippians 3:4–6). Since Paul was a native Hebrew, it is curious that he preached to the Greek Gentiles. He either became bilingual or relied upon translations. To the Greeks at Corinth, he wrote, "Unless you speak intelligible words with your tongue, how will anyone know what you are saying? You will just be speaking into the air. Undoubtedly there are all sorts of languages in the world, yet none of them is without meaning. If then I do not grasp the meaning of what someone is saying, I am a foreigner to the speaker, and the speaker is a foreigner to me. So it is with you. Since you are eager for gifts of the Spirit, try to excel in those that build up the church. For this reason, the one who speaks in a tongue should pray that they may interpret what they say" (1 Corinthians 14:8–12). Moreover, his letters probably were written in Hebrew or Aramaic or maybe even Latin and then translated to Greek somehow. There are differing opinions about his linguistics, all based on inference with no direct evidence.

Since Paul was persecuting Christians, the Christian Jews in Jerusalem were were afraid of him and did not believe that he was a disciple of Jesus (Acts 9:26). However, the record of his missionary zeal is unsurpassed by any of the original twelve. In fact, most of them just disappear into the fog of history, so it is to wonder why Jesus chose them to be "fishers of men" if Paul, who had no personal contact with him, was to be his primary missionary. And it is not for us to ask.

In the opening verses of his letter to the Romans, Paul provides a litany of his own apostolic appointment to preach among the Gentiles and his postconversion convictions about the risen Christ (Dr. Loren L. Johns).

- Paul described himself as a servant of Jesus Christ, having experienced an unforeseen sudden, startling change, due to all-powerful grace—not the fruit of his reasoning or thoughts (Galatians 1:12–15, 1; Corinthians 15:10)—having seen Christ as did the other apostles when Christ appeared to him (1 Corinthians 15:6) as he appeared to Peter, to James, to the twelve, after his Resurrection (1 Corinthians 9:01) called to be an apostle set apart for the Gospel of God.
- Paul described Jesus as
- having been promised by God beforehand through his prophets in the holy scriptures,
  - being the true Messiah and the Son of God,
  - having biological lineage from David ("according to the flesh") (Romans 1:3),
  - having been declared to be the Son of God in power according to the Spirit of Holiness by his resurrection from the dead,
  - being Jesus Christ our Lord, and
  - the One through whom we have received grace and apostleship to bring about the obedience of faith for the sake of his name among all the nations, "including you who are called to belong to Jesus Christ."

- Jesus
    - lives in Heaven,
    - is God's Son, and
    - would soon return.
- The Cross
    - Paul now believed that Jesus's death was a voluntary sacrifice that reconciled sinners with God. (Romans 5:6–10, Philippians 2:8)
- The Law
    - Paul now believed the law only reveals the extent of people's enslavement to the power of sin—a power that must be broken by belief in Christ. (Romans 3:20, 7:7–12)
- Gentiles
    - Paul had believed Gentiles were outside the covenant that God made with Israel.
    - He now believed Gentiles and Jews were united as the people of God in Christ Jesus. (Galatians 3:28)
- Circumcision
    - Paul had believed that circumcision was the rite through which males became part of Israel, an exclusive community of God's chosen people. (Philippians 3:3–5)
    - He now believed that neither circumcision nor uncircumcision means anything, but that the new creation is what counts in the sight of God (Galatians 6:15) and that this new creation is a work of Christ in the life of believers, making them part of the church of Christ, an inclusive community of Jews and Gentiles reconciled with God through faith. (Romans 6:4)
- Persecution
    - Paul had believed his violent persecution of the church to be an indication of his zeal for his pagan religion. (Philippians 3:6)
    - He now believed Jewish hostility toward the church was sinful opposition that would incur God's wrath

(1 Thessalonians 2:14–16). He believed he was halted by Christ when his fury was at its height (Acts 9:1–2). It was "through zeal" that he persecuted the Church (Philippians 3:6) and he obtained mercy because he had "acted ignorantly in unbelief" (1 Timothy 1:13). Nevertheless, he told the persecuted disciples of Christ to "be thankful in all things because this is the will of God for you" (1 Thessalonians 5:18).

- The Last Days
  - Paul had believed God's Messiah would put an end to the old age of evil and initiate a new age of righteousness.
  - He now believed this would happen in stages that had begun with the resurrection of Jesus, but the old age would continue until Jesus returns. (Romans 16:25, 1 Corinthians 10:11, Galatians 1:4)

Paul is critical both theologically and empirically of claims of moral or lineal superiority of Jews (Romans 2:16–26) while, conversely, strongly sustaining the notion of a special place for the Children of Israel in God's kingdom (Romans 9:11).

Christianity now is like an upside-down pyramid, with an ever-growing number of different factions all emanating from the writing of original sources, which is not available for study in this short summary. However, Paul laid down qualifications for bishops (a.k.a. overseers) and deacons to his ward of the church, Timothy, as follows:

> Whoever aspires to be an overseer (a.k.a. bishop) desires a noble task. Now the overseer is to be above reproach, faithful to his wife, temperate, self-controlled, respectable, hospitable, able to teach, not given to drunkenness, not violent but gentle, not quarrelsome, not a lover of money. He must be faithful to his wife and manage his household well and see that his children obey him, and he must do so in a manner worthy of full respect. If anyone

does not know how to manage his own family, how can he take care of God's church? He must not be a recent convert, or he may become conceited and fall under the same judgment as the devil. He must also have a good reputation with outsiders, so that he will not fall into disgrace and into the devil's trap.

An elder must be blameless, faithful to his wife, a man whose children believe] and are not open to the charge of being wild and disobedient. Since an overseer manages God's household, he must be blameless—not overbearing, not quick-tempered, not given to drunkenness, not violent, not pursuing dishonest gain. Rather, he must be hospitable, one who loves what is good, who is self-controlled, upright, holy and disciplined. He must hold firmly to the trustworthy message as it has been taught, so that he can encourage others by sound doctrine and refute those who oppose it. (Titus 1:6–9)

> In the same way, deacons are to be worthy of respect, sincere, not indulging in much wine, and not pursuing dishonest gain. They must keep hold of the deep truths of the faith with a clear conscience. They must first be tested; and then if there is nothing against them, let them serve as deacons. In the same way, the women are to be worthy of respect, not malicious talkers but temperate and trustworthy in everything. (1 Timothy 3:1–12)

Although Jesus commanded the disciples to go and baptize in the name of the Father, Son, and Holy Spirit to be "born again," this did not seem to be a high priority of Paul. Jesus said unless one is born of water and spirit, they cannot enter the kingdom of God (John 3:5–7). It seems that Paul did not get the message: "I thank God that I did not baptize any of you except Crispus and Gaius, so no one can say that you were baptized in my name. Yes, I also baptized the household of Stephanas; beyond that, I don't remember if I baptized anyone else. For Christ did not send me to baptize, but to preach the gospel" (1 Corinthians 1:14–17). Oh really? Then how were any of his converts "born again"? Recall he wrote, "If you declare that Christ is Lord and believe in your heart that God raised him from the dead, you will be saved" (Romans 10:9). No mention of baptism. Moreover, when the rich man asked Jesus what he must do for eternal life, Jesus told him to obey the commandments, sell all he had and give it to the poor, and follow him—without mentioning baptism (Matthew 19:16–24).

So there seems to be an important missing link here someplace in scripture about the role and requirement of baptism that leaves a chasm open for interpretation and proof texting. Jesus was baptized in the Jordan River by John the Baptist, so he is taken as an official role model, but the specific procedure is unclear. Some churches practice total immersion while others do not. Other common forms of baptism now include pouring water three times on the forehead, a method called "affusion." The Catholic Church requires baptism of infants by sprinkling, but a recent Vatican encyclical declared that infants who die without baptism will go directly to heaven. Again, they must not be born sinners for this to work. One could write a whole book about baptism, and some have. Could it be that Jesus was referring to human birth and death when he said "born of water and spirit"? For a complete discussion, visit https://en.wikipedia.org/wiki/Baptism.

Paul did not seem to be very big on human rights either when it came to slavery. He wrote,

> Slaves, obey your earthly masters in everything; and do it, not only when their eye is on you and to curry their favor, but with sincerity of heart and reverence for the Lord. Whatever you do, work at it with all your heart, as working for the Lord, not for human masters. (Colossians 3:21–23)

> All who are under the yoke of slavery should consider their masters worthy of full respect, so that

God's name and our teaching may not be slandered. Those who have believing masters should not show them disrespect just because they are fellow believers. Instead, they should serve them even better because their masters are dear to them as fellow believers and are devoted to the welfare of their slaves. Try to please them, not to talk back to them, and not to steal from them, but to show that they can be fully trusted, so that in every way they will make the teaching about God our Savior attractive. (1 Timothy 6:1–2, Titus 2:9–10)

Peter carried this instruction even further: "Slaves, in reverent fear of God submit yourselves to your masters, not only to those who are good and considerate, but also to those who are harsh. For it is commendable if someone bears up under the pain of unjust suffering because they are conscious of God. But how is it to your credit if you receive a beating for doing wrong and endure it? But if you suffer for doing good and you endure it, this is commendable before God. To this you were called, because Christ suffered for you, leaving you an example, that you should follow in his steps" (1 Peter 2:18–21).

Paul also thought everyone should obey the established government because it was ordained by God, without exception:

Let everyone be subject to the governing authorities, for there is no authority except that which God has established. The authorities that exist have been established by God. Consequently, whoever rebels against the authority is rebelling against what God has instituted, and those who do so will bring judgment on themselves. For rulers hold no terror for those who do right, but for those who do wrong. Do you want to be free from fear of the one in authority? Then do what is right and you will be commended. For the one in authority is God's servant for your good. But if you do wrong, be afraid, for rulers do not bear the sword for no reason. They are God's servants, agents of wrath to bring punishment on the wrongdoer. Therefore, it is necessary to submit to the authorities, not only because of possible punishment but also as a matter of conscience. This is also why you pay taxes, for the authorities are God's servants, who give their full time to governing. Give to everyone what you owe them: If you owe taxes, pay taxes; if revenue, then revenue; if respect, then respect; if honor, then honor. (Romans 13:1–7)

Scholars say he dictated this for transcribing by Tertius before he was imprisoned in Rome for disobeying authorities in Jerusalem (Romans 16:22) Honest.

This also was written by Apostle Peter: "Submit yourselves for the Lord's sake to every human authority: whether to the emperor, as the supreme authority, or to governors, who are sent by him to punish those who do wrong and to commend those who do right. For it is God's will that by doing good you should silence the ignorant talk of foolish people. Live as free people, but do not use your freedom as a cover-up for evil; live as God's slaves. Show proper respect to everyone, love the family of believers, fear God, honor the emperor" (1 Peter 2:13–17). Peter seems to forget the first commandment, which is to love the Lord, or thinks better of saying so.

However, when the apostles were ordered by the Jewish temple rulers, called the Sanhedrin, to stop preaching in the name of Jesus, Peter and the others replied, "We must obey God rather than human beings" (Acts 5:29). Tradition says that attitude got them all killed. Some say that Peter was crucified upside down at his request because he did not assume the same righteousness as Jesus.

We must recall here that Paul was both a Roman citizen and a Jewish Pharisee, both of which would dispose him to behave legally within the laws, both civil and biblical (Philippians 3:4–6). And Jesus said, "Give unto Caesar what is his and unto God what is his." But Jesus was not above breaking the laws of Moses every now and then, especially when it came to keeping the restrictions against working/healing on the Sabbath day, or stealing some grain from a field to eat along the way, or refusing to condemn a woman taken in adultery who was sentenced to stoning under the law: "The Sabbath was made for man and not man for the Sabbath…the Son of Man is Lord of the Sabbath" (Matthew 22:21, Matthew 12:2, Mark 2:27, Luke 6:2–5).

And yet Jesus seemed to imply that his followers should obey the teachers of the law: "Then Jesus said to the crowds and to his disciples: The teachers of the law and the Pharisees sit in Moses's seat. So you must be careful to do everything they tell you. But do not do what they do, for they do not practice what they preach" (Matthew 23:1–3). He also said some crazy stuff, like imagining adultery is the same as doing it, and if they ask, you should forgive those who harm you seventy-seven times because if you don't, "your Father in Heaven will not forgive you" (Matthew 6:14, Mark 11:25). I am not making this up.

Jesus granted some special places for women in his ministry, including the roles of Mary Magdalene and others. Paul seems to side with the paternalistic practices of the Jews in family life and their place in church to the point of telling women to keep silent and ask their husbands to explain anything they did not understand at home in private after the meeting. Peter seemed to agree with him in telling women to remain subordinate to their husbands, like Sarah did with Abraham, even calling him "my lord":

> Women should remain silent in the churches. They are not allowed to speak, but must be in submission, as the law says. If they want to inquire about something, they should ask their own husbands at home; for it is disgraceful for a woman to speak in the church. Wives, in the same way submit yourselves to your own husbands so that, if any of them do not believe the

> word, they may be won over without words by the behavior of their wives, when they see the purity and reverence of your lives. Your beauty should not come from outward adornment, such as elaborate hairstyles and the wearing of gold jewelry or fine clothes. Rather, it should be that of your inner self, the unfading beauty of a gentle and quiet spirit, which is of great worth in God's sight. (1 Corinthians 14:43–45)

> I also want the women to dress modestly, with decency and propriety, adorning themselves, not with elaborate hairstyles or gold or pearls or expensive clothes, but with good deeds, appropriate for women who profess to worship God. A woman should learn in quietness and full submission. I do not permit a woman to teach or to assume authority over a man; she must be quiet. For Adam was formed first, then Eve. And Adam was not the one deceived; it was the woman who was deceived and became a sinner. But women will be saved through childbearing—if they continue in faith, love and holiness with propriety. (1 Timothy 2: 9–13)

The Roman Catholic Church uses this proof text to prevent women from being ordained priests. But it does not seem to prevent the Episcopal Church or many Protestant denominations from ordaining women, citing other scriptures. Ladies, are you getting this?

It is more than a little odd that the same instruction to women is given in very similar words by Apostle Peter also (1 Peter 3:3–5). It appears that one copied from the other. Plus, he added, "Husbands, in the same way be considerate as you live with your wives, and treat them with respect as the weaker partner and as heirs with you of the gracious gift of life, so that nothing will hinder your prayers" (1 Peter

3:7). Paul says practically the same thing in Ephesians: "Husbands ought to love their wives as their own bodies. He who loves his wife loves himself. After all, no one ever hated their own body, but they feed and care for their body, just as Christ does the church— for we are members of his body. For this reason, a man will leave his father and mother and be united to his wife, and the two will become one flesh" (Ephesians 5:28–31). This is a quotation without attribution to Jesus and the book of Genesis (Genesis 2:24, Matthew 19:5, Mark 10:8). Since Paul wrote before the Gospels were written, he could only obtain it only from the Old Testament.

Muslims, Amish, and Mennonite churches seem to take these instructions seriously. Concerning married life, Paul recommended that single people remain unmarried as he was, so they can concentrate on serving God instead of their spouses, unless you cannot control your passions: "It is good for a man not to have sexual relations with a woman" (1 Corinthians 7:1). And widows would be happier if they remained single. Paul wrote no instructions to widowers, so we must do the best we can on our own. Besides, Jesus was returning soon so it did not pay to have a family—but if people could not control their passions, it is better to marry than to "burn": "An unmarried woman or virgin is concerned about the Lord's affairs: Her aim is to be devoted to the Lord in both body and spirit. But a married woman is concerned about the affairs of this world—how she can please her husband" (1 Corinthians 7:7–9, 33, 34).

On the other hand, former Fuller Seminary theologian J. R. Daniel Kirk (who was fired for being too progressive) finds evidence in Paul's letters of a much more inclusive view of women in the church. He writes that Romans 16 is a tremendously important witness to the important role of women in the early church. Paul praises Phoebe for her work as a deaconess and Junia who is described by Paul in scripture as being respected among the apostles (Romans 16:7). He also refers to "Priscilla and Aquila" numerous times as a married couple with thanks for their help in his ministry, even to housing him for eighteen months at one time. Moreover, scripture says, "There is neither Jew nor Gentile, neither slave nor free, nor is there male and female, for you are all one in Christ Jesus" (Galatians

3: 28). It is Kirk's observation that recent studies have led many scholars to conclude that the passage in 1 Corinthians 14 ordering women to be silent during worship was a later addition, apparently by a different author (maybe a Catholic bishop) and are not part of Paul's original letter to the Corinthians. Who knew? Since there are no surviving copies of the original letters, we cannot know what they contained or how they might be modified. While seeming to overlook the scriptural contradictions, several mainline denominations have authorized ordination of women in the late twentieth century: United Methodist, Presbyterian, American Baptist, Evangelical Lutheran, and Episcopal. Thus, Christian dogma is an evolving proposition apart from scriptures for progressive Christians. Is this the work of God or Satan? Or something bigger than both of them? I will discuss that possibility in the conclusion.

Then Paul really throws us a curve in his letter to Timothy: "The Spirit clearly says that in later times some will abandon the faith and follow deceiving spirits and things taught by demons. Such teachings come through hypocritical liars, whose consciences have been seared as with a hot iron. They forbid people to marry and order them to abstain from certain foods, which God created to be received with thanksgiving by those who believe and who know the truth. For everything God created is good, and nothing is to be rejected if it is received with thanksgiving, because it is consecrated by the word of God and prayer" (1 Timothy 4:1–5). Is this the same man who wrote the scriptures above? Some scholars say no.

Apostle Paul also seemed to have some disagreements with Apostle James on the subjects of faith and works. Faith is defined as "confidence/assurance in what we hope for and assurance about what we do not see" (Hebrews 11:1). "Consequently, faith comes from hearing the message, and the message is heard through the word about Christ" (Romans 10:17). Hope and faith are two key concepts in Christianity. Hope appears 97 times in the Old Testament and 73 times in the New Testament. German philosopher Ernest Bloch wrote in *The Principle of Hope* (1959) that while traditional religious beliefs in immortality or reincarnation are pure fantasy, they are also a manifestation of the utopian human hope. Hope is defined as an optimistic state of mind that is based on an expectation of positive outcomes with respect to events and circumstances in one's life or the world at large. As a verb, its definitions include "expect with confidence" and "to cherish a desire with anticipation." Being optimistic, in the hopeful sense of the word, is defined as expecting the best possible outcome from any given situation, that is, going to heaven for the righteous even though they suffer on earth.

Of course, the unrighteous who deny the Savior have no hope and must anticipate eternal suffering. Whether those who have not yet heard of the Savior are doomed is an unsettled debate. But those who hear the Word are without defense: "If I had not come and spoken to them, they would not be guilty of sin; but now they have no excuse for their sin" (John 15:22). It seems that ignorance of the law is an excuse, the opposite of modern jurisprudence. These variations in scriptures are very confusing, no? Once people hear the Word, it appears they must choose Christ, but whether they do or not appears to be the will of God (John 6:65). As the late great baseball catcher "Yogi" Berra once said, "When you come to a fork in the road, you have to take it." Everyone faces decisions in life that require choosing one road or another that once taken cannot be reversed, all in God's will, of course.

Faith is having a belief/trust without evidence, sort of like imagination or intuition, the ability to produce images, ideas, and sensations in the mind without any immediate input of the senses. In one form or another, the word "faith" appears 171 times in the Old Testament and 287 times in the New Testament. Whether faith is a choice or a gift cannot be concluded from the Bible. In some scriptures, it appears to be a free gift of grace from God; and in others, faith appears to be a willful decision on belief in magical thinking. Jesus said, "If you have faith as small as a mustard seed, you can say to this mountain, move from here to there, and it will move. Nothing will be impossible for you" (Matthew 17:20). Yes, Jesus said that—so the Bible says.

Sometimes faith is used as a noun as in having faith, and in some cases, it is a verb as in being faithful. "Without faith it is impossible to please God, because anyone who comes to him must believe that he exists and that he rewards those who earnestly seek him." (Hebrews 11:6). Jesus also declared it was their own faith in him that obtained the healing that the sick received, and he told his disciples if they believed it. They would receive anything they asked for in prayer (Matthew 21:22; Matthew 9:22, 29, 15:28). In some discussions, faith is presented as fruit of the spirit or a form of grace to those who believe. Faith is defined as being a positive response to what God has already provided by grace. In other words, faith is your positive response to God's grace. Faith is tested in the smelting fires of trials, and yet it is God who gives us the grace to stand fast in the day of trouble. As grace is poured out upon grace, so faith increases as a believer grows in grace and matures in the faith.

It seems like faith can work in reverse also: "Early in the morning, as Jesus was on his way back to the city, he was hungry. Seeing a fig tree by the road, he went up to it but found nothing on it except leaves. Then he said to it, May you never bear fruit again! Immediately the tree withered. When the disciples saw this, they were amazed. How did the fig tree wither so quickly? they asked. Jesus replied, Truly I tell you, if you have faith and do not doubt, not only can you do what was done to the fig tree, but also you can say to this mountain, Go, throw yourself into the sea, and it will be done. Therefore, I tell you, whatever you ask for in prayer, believe that you have received it, and it will be yours. If you believe, you will receive whatever you ask for in prayer" (Matthew 21:18–22, Mark 11:24). In other words, your belief creates your reality, and it can control the world around you. Believe that notion and you might be diagnosed as mentally ill. And yet, some new age churches rely on such scripture as their basic doctrine, calling it "the law of attraction." Their theme seems to be "Think you are the way you want to be, and soon you will be the way you think," which can be traced back to "mind cures" in the nineteenth century. Without challenging the veracity of this scripture, I think using it that way is a blatant example of proof texting because another scripture says, "Therefore, you ought to say, if the Lord wills, we shall live and do this or that" (James 4:13–15). So which scripture are you gonna believe? Do you have a choice?

Such potential proof texting is a common error of scripture interpretation. Opportunities occur throughout the New Testament for proof texting around the word "believe." Jesus plainly was addressing the people in his immediate audience above with the word "you" in second person. If he meant to state an overall generalization, the scripture would need to use a word in third person such as "anyone" or "everyone" and "whoever." Consider these examples: "Whoever believes in him is not condemned, but whoever does not believe stands condemned already because they have not believed in the name of God's one and only Son. (John 3:18, 36) "Without faith it is impossible to please God, because anyone who comes to him must believe that he exists and that he rewards those who earnestly seek him. (Hebrews 11:6) But, do not forget that scripture says such belief is a gift of God and not of the individual will. "For Jesus had known from the beginning which of them did not believe and who would betray him. He went on to say, this is why I told you that no one can come to me unless the Father has enabled them." (John 6:65) You cannot avoid your destiny.

Believers of this kind of proof text about faith can feel very frustrated and disappointed when it does not work for them. However, sometimes it works as when a person sees their wishes or prayers fulfilled, which only adds credence to the mystery of God's will. Someone always wins the lottery in life, which prompts many people to gamble the grocery money for a chance of winning, no matter how remote it is. But, it is not very helpful if you are living in a refugee camp or dying of cancer to depend on faith alone, although some people insist on doing so. Therefore, you must ask yourself while reading scriptures, "What has that got to do with me?"

Moreover, James, the assumed brother of Jesus, wrote conflicting instructions, if indeed he was the writer: "Is anyone among you sick? Let them call the elders of the church to pray over them and anoint them with oil in the name of the Lord. And the prayer offered in faith will make the sick person well; the Lord will raise them up" (James 5:14–15). This scripture is contrasted with, "What good is it, my brothers and sisters, if someone claims to have faith but has no deeds? Can such faith save them? Suppose a brother or a sister is without clothes and daily food. If one of you says to them, go in peace; keep warm and well fed, but does nothing about their physical needs, what good is it? In the same way, faith by itself, if it is not accompanied by action, is dead. But someone will say, You have faith; I have deeds. Show me your faith without deeds, and I will show you my faith by my deeds… As the body without the spirit is dead, so faith without deeds is dead" (James 2:14–18, 2:26). Indeed, Jesus declared in one parable that charity was a prerequisite to avoiding the flames of hell: "Depart from me, you who are cursed, into the eternal fire prepared for the devil and his angels. For I was hungry and you gave me nothing to eat, I was thirsty and you gave me nothing to drink" (Matthew 25:40–42).

To which Paul replied, "There are different kinds of service, but the same Lord. There are different kinds of working, but in all of them and in everyone it is the same God at work." He expands on that idea: "Now to each one the manifestation of the Spirit is given for the common good. To one there is given through the Spirit a message of wisdom, to another a message of knowledge by means of the same Spirit, to another faith by the same Spirit, to another gifts of healing by that one Spirit, to another miraculous powers, to another prophecy, to another distinguishing between spirits, to another speaking in different kinds of tongues (aka languages) and to still another the interpretation of tongues. All these are the work of one and the same Spirit, and he distributes them to each one, just as he determines" (1 Corinthians 12:5–11). Paul declared his faith was secured by knowledge: "I know whom I have believed, and am convinced that he is able to guard what I have entrusted to him until that day" (2 Timothy 1:12). It seems people do not really have much control over the work of the Spirit. They just must live with whatever gifts they are given, or not. All in God's will of course.

Whatever the challenges were in the early church of Christ, Paul seemed to think the future benefits were worth the burdens involved in membership and service. He had certain privileges as a Hebrew from the tribe of Benjamin, a Pharisee, and a Roman citizen, that he was willing to leave behind (Philippians 3:5). During his later days while chained and imprisoned in Rome, he could still feel emancipated from the old while looking forward to the new: "But whatever were gains to me I now consider loss for the sake of Christ. What is more, I consider everything a loss because of the surpassing worth of knowing Christ Jesus my Lord, for whose sake I have lost all things. I consider them garbage, that I may gain Christ and be found in him, not having a righteousness of my own that comes from (obeying) the law, but that which is through faith in Christ—the righteousness that comes from God on the basis of faith. I want to know Christ—yes, to know the power of his resurrection and participation in his sufferings, becoming like him in his death, and so, somehow, attaining to the resurrection from the dead" (Philippians 3:7–11).

Paul made a powerful argument for believing in the resurrection of Jesus and resurrection of the dead: "And if Christ has not been raised, our preaching is useless and so is your faith. For if the dead are not raised, then Christ has not been raised either. And if Christ has not been raised, your faith is futile; you are still in your sins. If only for this life we have hope in Christ, we are to be pitied more than all people. But Christ has indeed been raised from the dead. For since death came through a man, the resurrection of the dead comes also through a man. For as in Adam all die, so in Christ all will be made alive" (1 Corinthians, chapter 15).

(*This chapter contains nine footnotes of sources in the Old Testament and elsewhere, indicating the writer was a very learned author. This is a feature that flows throughout the Gospels. I wonder how the writers were able to reference so many scriptures in the Old Testament, or if they were inserted later by educated scribes. Some scholars have discovered later additions even unto the fourteenth century that are not in older Vulgate manuscripts—all in God's will, of course.*)

Perhaps the best of Paul is the description and value he gave to the discussion of love:

> If I speak in the tongues of men or of angels, but do not have love, I am only a resounding gong or a clanging cymbal. If I have the gift of prophecy and can fathom all mysteries and all knowledge, and if I have a faith that can move mountains,

but do not have love, I am nothing. If I give all I possess to the poor and give over my body to hardship that I may boast, but do not have love, I gain nothing. Love is patient, love is kind. It does not envy, it does not boast, it is not proud. It does not dishonor others, it is not self-seeking, it is not easily angered, it keeps no record of wrongs. Love does not delight in evil but rejoices with the truth. It always protects, always trusts, always hopes, always perseveres.

Love never fails. But where there are prophecies, they will cease; where there are tongues, they will be stilled; where there is knowledge, it will pass away. For we know in part and we prophesy in part, but when completeness comes, what is in part disappears. When I was a child, I talked like a child, I thought like a child, I reasoned like a child. When I became a man, I put the ways of childhood behind me. For now we see only a reflection as in a mirror; then we shall see face to face. Now I know in part; then I shall know fully, even as I am fully known. And now these three remain: faith, hope and love. But the greatest of these is love. (1 Corinthians 13)

One may wonder why Jesus did not include in the "Sermon on the Mount" a blessing on anyone who finds such an experience of love because I think it surpasses all the other blessings in the beatitudes. (But we must note the word "love" is translated as "charity" in the King James Version of the Bible. To give unconditionally, that is love.)

The word "love" appears 310 times in the King James Bible, 348 times in the New American Standard Bible, 686 times in the New International Version, and 538 times in the New Revised Standard Version. The extremely varied numbers for the usage of the word are due in part to translation. The Greek language used in the Bible has at least four English words to describe the various aspects of love, both as a noun and as a verb. Three of these four were used in the New Testament. "Phileo" is a comradely affection toward someone we really like or feel allied with. "Storgay" refers to loving one's family relatives. It is a term that is used only two times in scripture and only as a compound. "Eros," used to describe a sexual or romantic type of love in the Greek, is not found in scripture, but may be inferred mostly in Solomon's Song of Songs, which you will not likely read in church. "Agape," which is the deepest love, also means doing good things for another person unconditionally, as when Jesus said there is no greater love than to give your life for your friends (John 15:13). Lyrics to a popular song say, "You're nobody 'til somebody loves you. You're nobody 'til somebody cares…so find yourself somebody to love."

How these various forms of love might exist in a church could be explored in another book because they rarely are discussed. As to the temptations to engage in sexual pleasure, St. Augustine of Hippo (354–430 CE) prayed, "Lord, give me chastity and continence, but not yet." And Lord Chesterfield observed about sex, "The position is unseemly, the pleasure is momentary, and the consequences are abominable." Celibacy among Orthodox Catholic priests was mandated in the eleventh century although it was implied and debated from the fourth century based upon a balanced reading of scriptures (Matthew 19:12, 1 Corinthians 7:25). Considering all the alleged sexual abuse by priests, one may wonder if this is such a good idea.

I suppose the bottom line for Paul is this:

> Nevertheless, each person should live as a believer in whatever situation the Lord has assigned to them, just as God has called them. This is the rule I lay down in all the churches. What I mean, brothers and sisters, is that the time is short. From now on those who have wives should live as if they do not; those who mourn, as if they did not; those who are happy, as if they were not; those who buy something, as if it were not theirs

to keep; those who use the things of the world, as if not engrossed in them. For this world in its present form is passing away. (1 Corinthians 7:29–31)

It seems that the writer spoke out of both sides of his mouth, does it not? When you are called, stay as you are but live as you are not. And by the way, the world as it is still is here two thousand years later even though countless individuals among all life species have come and gone. Whew! A complete dissection of the diverse instructions of Paul would need another book. (To read more of his instructions to the incipient churches, refer to appendix B.)

Reconciling Jehovah and God

There is an ongoing struggle to reconcile the god Jehovah or Yahweh of the Old Testament—the one he created who destroyed the enemies of Israel and kept forgiving their sins and restoring the covenant as the chosen people—with God the Father in the New Testament, the one who loved the sinful world, which he created so much he gave his only son to save it. The difficulty turns on the applications of love in the affairs of humankind and their relationship to the Creator. In the Old Testament, Yahweh is depicted as jealous, angry, judgmental, and vindictive. Love is directed from the chosen people to God in the Old Testament, while in the New Testament love is directed from God to all people whom he has chosen to believe in him. Here are some examples:

> Hear, O Israel: The LORD our God, the LORD is one. Love the LORD your God with all your heart and with all your soul and with all your strength. These commandments that I give you today are to be on your hearts… You shall have no other Gods before me… For the Lord your God is a consuming fire, a jealous God. (Deuteronomy 4:24, 5:7, 6:4–6)

This is what the Lord of hosts has to say: I will punish what Amalek did to Israel when he barred his way as he was coming up from Egypt. Go, now, attack Amalek, and deal with him and all that he has under the ban. Do not spare him, but kill men and women, children and infants, oxen and sheep, camels and asses. (1 Samuel 15:2–3)

You do not delight in sacrifice, or I would bring it; you do not take pleasure in burnt offerings. My sacrifice, O God, is a broken spirit; a broken and contrite heart you, God, will not despise. (Psalm 51:16–18)

I will make Mount Seir utterly desolate, killing off all who try to escape and any who return. I will fill your mountains with the dead. Your hills, your valleys, and your streams will be filled with people slaughtered by the sword. I will make you desolate forever. Your cities will never be rebuilt. Then you will know that I am the LORD. (Ezekiel 35:7–9)

Anyone who is captured will be run through with a sword. Their little children will be dashed to death right before their eyes. Their homes will be sacked, and their wives will be raped by the attacking hordes. For I will stir up the Medes against Babylon, and no amount of silver or gold will buy them off. The attacking armies will shoot down the young people with arrows. They will have no mercy on helpless babies and will show no compassion for the children. (Isaiah 13:15–18)

O Babylon, you will be destroyed. Happy is the one who pays you back for what you have done

> to us. Happy is the one who takes your babies and smashes them against the rocks! (Psalms 137:8–9)

> And now, Israel, what does the Lord your God ask of you but to fear the Lord your God, to walk in obedience to him, to love him, to serve the Lord your God with all your heart and with all your soul. (Deuteronomy 10:12)

Actually, the first commandment is to love God with all your heart, soul, and mind, or something like that.

Compare those Old Testament scriptures with these words of love in the New Testament:

> God so loved the world he gave his only son so whoever believes in him will not perish but have everlasting life. (John 3:16)

> But I say to you who hear, love your enemies, do good to those who hate you, bless those who curse you, pray for those who mistreat you. Whoever hits you on the cheek, offer him the other also; and whoever takes away your coat, do not withhold your shirt from him either. Give to everyone who asks of you, and whoever takes away what is yours, do not demand it back. If a (*Roman soldier*) commands you to carry his pack for a mile, carry it for two. (Matthew 5:41, NLT; Luke 6:27–30)

> Dear friends, let us love one another, for love comes from God. Everyone who loves has been born of God and knows God. Whoever does not love does not know God, because God is love. This is how God showed his love among us: He

sent his one and only Son into the world that we might live through him. This is love: not that we loved God, but that he loved us and sent his Son as an atoning sacrifice for our sins. Dear friends, since God so loved us, we also ought to love one another. No one has ever seen God; but if we love one another, God lives in us and his love is made complete in us. (1 John 4:7–12)

I have loved you with an everlasting love, and constant is my affection for you. (Matthew 28:20, Jeremiah 31:3)

Greater love has no one than this: that one lays down one's life for his friends. (John: 15:13)

Marcion of Sinope (85–160CE) developed a solution to this seeming dilemma in the first century by declaring the god of the Old Testament to be an impostor, a Demiurge, not worthy of worshipping, and the whole Old Testament is not worth reading. The Old and New Testaments, Marcion argued, cannot be reconciled to each other. The code of conduct advocated by Moses was an eye for an eye, but Christ set this precept aside by instructing to love your enemies and judge not that you may not be judged. Elisha had children eaten by bears; Christ said, "Let the little children come to me." Joshua stopped the sun in its path in order to continue the slaughter of his enemies; but Paul quoted Christ as commanding, "Let not the sun go down on your wrath."

In the Old Testament, divorce was permitted and so was polygamy; but in the New Testament, neither is allowed. Moses enforced the Jewish Sabbath and law; Christ freed believers from both. Marcion saw the father of Jesus as the only true God. He created his own form of scriptural canon concentrated on the Gospel of Luke and the epistles of Paul, and he founded a movement that existed for several centuries before it faded into history, long after he was excommunicated for heresy by his own father who was a bishop of

Sinope. But Marcion's argument was so iron clad that Tertullian, second-century father of the church, required five volumes to refute it.

For some Christians, the obvious problems of the Old Testament and the contrasting appeal of Jesus are such that they identify themselves as modern-day Marcionites. They follow his solution in keeping the New Testament as sacred scripture while rejecting the Old Testament canon and practices. A term sometimes used for these groups is "New Testament Christians." There is some merit in disconnecting the two testaments because they seem to discuss two different kinds of gods. Love in the Old Testament is focused on man's toward God, and in the New Testament it is focused on God's toward man. One could make a study on the biblical use of the word "love" alone as this discussion obviously is oversimplified. Marcion was credible because there is no way to reconcile the differences, unless there is some superior power that created both of them, which leads to the principle of necessary opposites and the GOD above Gods proposed by Paul Tillich.

It also would be interesting to study the word "power," which appears 200 times in that Old Testament and 135 times in the New Testament. "But you belong to God, my children, and have defeated the false prophets, because the spirit who is in you is more powerful than the spirit in those who belong to the world" (1 John 4:4 GNT). Jesus declared he has overcome the world. "I have told you these things, so that in me you may have peace. In this world you will have trouble. But take heart! I have overcome the world" (John 16:33). However, the Bible also says the world presently is ruled by Satan who will not be destroyed until the end of this dispensation (Revelation 12:9). Reconciling these scriptures is far beyond the limited scope of this work, but it goes to illustrate the issues and challenges in applying what the Bible says in any practical way to our lives today without proof texting scriptures.

Perhaps there is some resolution between the Old and New Testaments in the form of a new covenant that replaces the old, or maybe not. "Christ is the mediator of a new covenant. Apostle Paul wrote as follows to the church in Rome.

"To all in Rome who are loved by God and are <u>called to be his holy people</u>: Grace and peace to you from God our Father and from the Lord Jesus Christ. And you also are among those Gentiles who <u>are called to belong to Jesus Christ.</u> (Romans 1:6-7) To the Colossians he wrote, "Therefore, a<u>s God's chosen people</u>, holy and dearly loved, clothe yourselves with compassion, kindness, humility, gentleness and patience." (Colossians 3:12) He also wrote, "For we know, brothers and sisters loved by God, that <u>he has chosen you</u>, because our gospel came to you not simply with words but also with power, (1Thessalonians 1:4-5) This translation appears the same in fifty-two of the sixty English versions provided in the Biblegateway.com. The only plausible alternative is to substitute the word "invited" for the words "called" or "chosen."

But, the problem remains. Whether to be called or invited, it seems that some are, and some are not. Jesus told his twelve apostles, "You did not choose me, <u>I chose/called you</u>." (John 15:16) "For many are invited, but few are chosen." (Matthew 22:14) "If you belonged to the world, it would love you as its own. As it is, you do not belong to the world, but <u>I have chosen you</u> out of the world. That is why the world hates you." (John 15:19) As the Jews were chosen by God for the Old Covenant so it seems Christians were chosen by God for the New Covenant. How and if this is applied to our age is unknown.

One disciple, Thomas, was hard to convince that Jesus had risen. He wasn't asked to believe without evidence on the basis of testimony by the other disciples alone. Jesus permitted him to examine the wounds to convince him. The reason John gives for recounting these events is that what he saw is sufficient evidence: "Then Jesus told him, Because you have seen me, you have believed; blessed are those who have not seen and yet have believed. Jesus did many other miraculous signs in the presence of his disciples… But these are written that you may believe that Jesus is the Christ, the son of God, and that believing you might have (eternal) life in his name" (John 20:24–39). However, recall that Jesus declared no one can come to him unless the Father calls/enables them (John 6:65). The ascension of Jesus into heaven gets the most attention in the book of Mark, which some scholars doubt was part of the original manuscript. The books of Matthew and John do not describe it at all. It is abbreviated in the Gospel of Luke and mentioned briefly in the book of Acts. So the story of Jesus ends differently depending on which book you read.

Eschatology

(*Wikipedia*) Just as the Bible describes the beginning of creation, so does it also describe the ending. If the description of the beginning is fantastic, the description of the ending is even more so. The final chapter of life on earth and its replacement with the everlasting dictatorship under Jesus as the omnipotent judge are the subjects of two books, the book of Daniel in the Old Testament and the book of Revelation in the New Testament. This commentary relates to the nature of these books rather than their specific content, as that is subject to many different interpretations that have even the scholars debating endlessly. However, the subject deserves a brief overall discussion.

History is divided into (typically seven) "dispensations" where God tests man's obedience differently. These dispensations are depicted as seven different churches. The present church dispensation concerns Christians (mainly Gentiles) and is a parenthesis to God's main plan of dealing with and blessing his chosen people, the Jews. Because of their rejection of Jesus, Jewish sovereignty over the promised earthly kingdom of Jerusalem and Palestine was postponed from the time of Christ's first coming until prior to or just after his second coming when most or all Jews will embrace him as the King of Kings. There will be an instantaneous departure (a.k.a. Rapture) of the Church (some say for a thousand years) followed by a great tribulation of seven (or three-and-a-half) years' duration during which the Antichrist will rule and Armageddon, the final battle between good and evil, will occur. Then Jesus will return visibly to earth and reestablish the nation of Israel; the Jewish temple will be rebuilt at Jerusalem and the temple mount, possibly in place of the Muslim Dome of the Rock. Christ and the people of Israel will reign in Jerusalem for a thousand years, followed by the last judgment and a new heaven and new earth (Revelation 21:1).

The Bible is not clear about the details, so there are many different interpretations. No one but God knows when these events will occur, not even Jesus, but then again maybe he does for those who believe he is God. "But about that day or hour no one knows, not even the angels in heaven, nor the Son, but only the Father" (Matthew 24:36). Apostle Paul wrote, "Now, brothers and sisters, about times and dates we do not need to write to you, for you know very well that the day of the Lord will come like a thief in the night. While people are (seeking) peace and safety, destruction will come on them suddenly, as labor pains on a pregnant woman, and they will not escape" (1 Thessalonians 5:1). On the other hand, Jesus said his generation would not pass away until all these things would happen (Matthew 24:34–35). (For more details, browse *Christian Zionism*.) Science says the earth and all the planets will be consumed in fire about four billion years hence as the sun runs out of hydrogen and its nuclear fusion is converted into a giant red implosion. But here we are talking about what the Bible says and that only.

The primary source for these prophecies is the book of Revelation, said to be written by the Apostle John while he was in exile on the Isle of Patmos. Its prologue says, "The revelation from Jesus Christ, which God gave him to show his servants what must soon take place. He made it known by sending his angel to his servant John, who testifies to everything he saw—that is, the word of God and the testimony of Jesus Christ. Blessed is the one who reads aloud the words of this prophecy, and blessed are those who hear it and take to heart what is written in it, because the time is near (Revelation 1:1,9).

There are approximately 300 surviving Greek manuscripts of Revelation. While the Codex Vaticanus does not include it, the other major manuscripts that do are the Codex Sinaiticus (fourth century), Codex Alexandrinus (fifth century), and Codex Ephraemi Rescriptus (fifth century). Divisions in the book seem to be marked by the repetition of key phrases, by the arrangement of subject matter into blocks, and around its Christological passages. Much use is made of significant numbers, especially the number seven, which represented perfection according to ancient numerology.

The Revelation opens as follows: "John, To the seven churches in the province of Asia: Grace and peace to you from him who is, and who was, and who is to come, and from the seven spirits before his throne, and from Jesus Christ, who is the faithful witness, the firstborn from the dead, and the ruler of the kings of the earth… On the Lord's Day I was in the Spirit, and I heard behind me a loud voice like a trumpet, which said, write on a scroll what you see and send it to the seven churches: to Ephesus, Smyrna, Pergamum, Thyatira, Sardis, Philadelphia and Laodicea… Blessed is the one who reads aloud the words of this prophecy, and blessed are those who hear it and take to heart what is written in it, because the time is near… I am the Alpha and the Omega, says the Lord God, who is, and who was, and who is to come, the Almighty" (Revelation 1:4, 8–10).

Revelation has a wide variety of interpretations, ranging from the simple message that we should have faith that God will prevail ("symbolic interpretation"), to complex end-time scenarios ("futurist interpretation"), to the views of critics who deny any spiritual value to Revelation at all and place it in the realm of myth and legend. The number seven is featured as it was assumed to be a perfect number in numerology. In some interpretations, a time of tribulation is coming when Satan will be given full reign over the world, which must be shortened to seven years to avoid total destruction. Jesus will return eventually to rout out Satan and all his angels in a final battle of "Armageddon," after which there will be set up a new heaven and a new earth under the absolute reign of Jesus as King eternal. The number 666 as the mark of "the beast" and 144,000 as the number "who were sealed" are given prominence also. Depending on the interpretation, the church, both living and dead, will be removed (raptured) before, during, or after the great tribulation.

During the 1970s, belief in the Rapture became popular, in part because of the books of Hal Lindsey, including *The Late Great Planet Earth*, which has reportedly sold between 15 million and 35 million copies, and the movie *A Thief in the Night*, which based its title on the scriptural reference, 1 Thessalonians 5:2. Lindsey proclaimed that the Rapture was imminent, based on world conditions at the time. In 1995, the doctrine of the pretribulation rapture was popularized by Tim LaHaye's *Left Behind* series of books (actually written by Jerry B. Jenkins). The series includes twelve titles in the adult series, as well as juvenile novels, audio books, video games, devotionals, and graphic novels. The books have been very popular, with total sales surpassing 65 million copies as of July 2016. Such is the power of the human imagination and the need for some certainty about the future, which is indefinitely uncertain. Nothing illustrates this more than wondering how a politician will act after the election, regardless of which side you support.

Most Christian interpretations of Revelation fall into one or more of the following categories:

- Historicism, which sees in Revelation a broad view of history
- Preterism, in which Revelation mostly refers to the events of the apostolic era (first century) or, at the latest, the fall of the Roman Empire
- Amillennialism, which contends that the final millennium has already begun and is identical with the current church age
- Futurism, which believes that Revelation describes future events. Modern believers in this interpretation are often called "millennialists"
- Idealism/Allegoricalism, which holds that Revelation does not refer to actual people or events, but is an allegory of the spiritual path and the ongoing struggle between good and evil in which good will ultimately vanquish evil

The book of Daniel, is the other book on the apocalypse, a literary genre in which a heavenly reality is revealed to a human recipient. The prophecy of apocalypses occurred commonly from 300 BCE to AD 100, not only among Jews and Christians, but also among Greeks, Romans, Persians, and Egyptians. Such works are characterized by visions, symbolism, an otherworldly mediator, with emphasis on cosmic events, angels, and demons. The message of the book of Daniel is that, just as the God of Israel saved Daniel and his friends from their enemies, like protecting them in the lion's den, so he would save all Israel in their present oppression as the Diaspora in Babylonia. The book is filled with monsters, angels, and numerology, drawn from a wide range of sources, both biblical and nonbiblical. While some Christian interpreters have viewed these tales as predicting events in the New Testament—the Son of God, the Son of Man, Christ, and the Antichrist —the book's intended audience is the Jews of the second century BCE.

Daniel, the book's hero, is a representative apocalyptic seer, the recipient of divine revelation. He has learned the wisdom of the Babylonian magicians and surpassed them because his god is the true source of knowledge; he is one of the wise ones who have the task of teaching righteousness and whose number may include the authors of the book itself. The book is also an eschatology, as the divine revelation concerns the end of the present age, a predicted moment in which God will intervene in history to usher in the final kingdom. It will be a time of great distress, but all those whose names are written in the book of life will be delivered. Multitudes who sleep in the dust of the earth will awake, some to everlasting life, others to shame and everlasting contempt; those who are wise will shine like the brightness of the heavens, and those who lead many to righteousness, like the stars for ever and ever. So says Daniel. (*Wikipedia*)

Jesus declared, "Truly I tell you, this generation will certainly not pass away until all these things have happened. Heaven and earth will pass away, but my words will never pass away" (Matthew 24:34–35). He was wrong on the former and possibly right on the latter. The Bible gives confusing details of the end-time, but it seems that God's kingdom will be governed by justice and righteousness and that the tables will be turned on Satan and his angels and all who have cooperated with them: "The Son of Man will send out his angels, and they will weed out of his kingdom everything that causes sin and all who do evil. They will throw them into the blazing furnace, where there will be weeping and gnashing of teeth. Then the righteous will shine like the sun in the kingdom of their father. Whoever has ears, let them hear" (Matthew 13: 41–43).

In the end, the chosen ones will enjoy life eternal in a perfect utopia with the Lord and all the others will suffer eternity in hell. Apostle Paul expected these events to occur within his lifetime: "For the Lord himself will come down from heaven, with a loud command, with the voice of the archangel and with the trumpet call of God, and the dead in Christ will rise first. After that, we who are still alive and are left will be caught up together with them in the clouds to meet the Lord in the air. And so we will be with the Lord forever" (1 Thessalonians 4:17). Those Christians who look forward to this time in the perpetual uncertain future seem to embrace eternal life under the complete and total benevolent dictatorship of Jesus Christ. In fact, scriptures in the New Testament repeat forty-four times the promise of eternal life is through belief in Jesus as Lord and Savior. Jesus declared, "My sheep listen to my voice; I know them, and they follow me. I give them eternal life, and they shall never perish; no one will snatch them out of my hand. My Father, <u>who has given them to me</u>, is greater than all and no one can snatch them out of my Father's hand" (John 10:27–29). World peace will come at last in the Kingdom of God under the one-world government that is so vehemently opposed by many present- day mainline Christians. Thus endeth this commentary on the Bible.

> The biblical description of the end times is different from that which science now assumes. Our sun, which powers the earth from 93 million miles away precisely to sustain life, is a nuclear fusion reaction using hydrogen as its fuel. This fuel will be consumed gradually over time until about 3.4 billion years hence when the sun will burn out and collapse into a "Red Giant" that will expand and consume the earth in a fiery cataclysm. If the past history of life on earth is projected forward, living species could change more than we can imagine before then.

A New Pathway to Enlightenment

Life is not an easy matter. You cannot live through it without falling into frustration and cynicism unless you have before you a great idea which raises you above all kinds of perfidy and baseness.

—Leon Trotsky

It is written: Man shall not live on bread alone, but on every word that comes from the mouth of God.

—Matthew 4:4

And we know that in all things God works for the good of those who love him, who have been called according to his purpose.

—Romans 8:28

What good fortune for those in power that (many) people do not think.

—Adolf Hitler

Is this, then, true or merely vain fantasy?

—Euripedes

Hope is the worst of all evils for it prolongs the torments of man.

—Friedrich Nietzsche

Religion is the opiate of the masses.

—Karl Marx

No doubt, there are many more scriptural references that could be added to this commentary to help illustrate this conclusion, but those discussed herein are sufficient to make the point. Proof texting the Bible can lead to false conclusions, and if you do not proof text the Bible, much of it makes no sense due to its confusion and contradictions. Apostle Paul wrote, "God is not the author of confusion" (1 Corinthians 14:33), yet never has a book produced more confusion than the Bible. It is all a matter of personal interpretation, and one is as good as another.

When you consider that Christianity merely is one of the great religions of the world among hundreds, and it was carved up into many denominations after the Reformation, one must deal with the existential why—why are there so many different religions, and why has Christianity survived and grown through two millennia even though it is fatally flawed in both content and practice? The Graduate Theological Union library in Berkeley, California, claims it contains files on more than 900 different religions in the United State (www.gtu.edu). (Actually, Islam, which means submission to God, is the fastest-growing religion in the world and is expected to equal Christianity by 2050. Muslims believe everything, good and bad, is decreed by God, a.k.a. Allah.) Even professional scholars often disagree on interpretations of various Bible scriptures—as shown by the books listed in the bibliography. In spite of its many flaws, inconsistencies, and downright contradictions, many people turn to the Bible generation after generation, seeking something they think can be found in it worth making the effort. Why do they do that?

It seems that many people have an insatiable need to feel loved by God. The only plausible explanation must be some power greater than any other is driving this human phenomenon. This discovery may be like Albert Einstein said he felt after discovering the new laws of physics. It was like the earth was removed from under him and there was no firm place on which to stand. C. G. Jung described his similar reaction to the spiritual crisis of his life which led him through a decade of self-discovery out of a black pit of despair. He wrote in *Memories, Dreams, Reflections*, "Suddenly it was as though the ground literally gave way beneath my feet, and I plunged down into dark depths." (1989, p. 203) Only after he had a near death experience during a heart attack could he say, "I don't have to believe because I know." Others who claim a similar near-death experience also describe a resulting inner peace and confidence in the afterlife

Those who criticize the Bible without proposing any solution to its difficulties leave Christians on similar quicksand of indefinite uncertainty. Is there any possible alternative, or are we witnessing an evolutionary transition among the faithful from the past into the future, a future that accommodates the unknown and, possibly, the unknowable? This is what someone said is the finite trying to understand the infinite. With passage of time, empires and civilizations come and go as though some power greater than any individual leaders seems to be directing the affairs of all living creatures on earth, from ants to elephants, including *Homo sapiens*. It seems like some power yet to be explained is driving human history in both secular and religious affairs.

Perhaps there is an explanation of that power, which accommodates the Bible as well as all other religious holy books. Science postulates the existence of undetectable dark matter and dark energy based on observable cosmic behavior, so why not such a revelation based on inference from evolution of religious behavior? Could not human creativity come up with a solution to all the confusion in the Bible? Dr. Jung called it the active imagination that drives all human progress. The late great scientist Albert Einstein thought that imagination is more important than knowledge: "The intellect has little to do on the road to discovery. There comes a leap of consciousness, call it intuition or what you will, and the solution comes to you and you don't know how or why. The intuitive mind is a sacred gift and the rational mind is a faithful servant. We have created a society that honors the servant and has forgotten the gift." Jung said intuition is perception through the subconscious. He saw a danger to mankind in overconcentration on the technology-based society absent a necessary balance in the arts. Napoleon Bonaparte (1769–1821) concluded, "Imagination rules the world."

Growing Beyond the Bible

The Bible has served a basic need of humans to believe in something that is transformative and provides solace facing the indefinite uncertainty about a future that is unpredictable. However, the basic problem with Christianity is that very few people can imagine and accept that God causes destruction of his/its own creation because they are taught all human behavior and suffering are caused by their inherited will to sin. That assumption seems to negate free will before we are born. We may not be able to see God, but we can "his" creation, and a lot of it stinks pretty badly. He creates laws and causes people to break them, so he can save some at his own discretion. Think about the earthquakes, hurricanes, tornadoes, diseases, wars, murders, bankruptcies, etc.: "I, the Lord, do all these things" (Isaiah 45:7). Even the so-called "accidents" seem to be inevitable when you consider all the causes that go into causing them as links in an unbreakable chain all the way back to the First Cause. Causal determinism proposes that there is an unbroken chain of prior occurrences stretching back to the origin of the universe.

Modern smart cell phones can be linked back to the personal computer created by Steve Jobs (1955–2011) to the microchip invented by Robert Noyce (1927–1990) and Ted Hoff (1937–) to the transistor invented by William Shockley (1910–1989) to information science developed by Claude Shannon (1916–2001) to digital math developed by self-taught George Boole (1815–1864) and discovery of fractal geometry. Modern digital video can be linked back to invention of the phonograph and his moving pictures by Thomas Edison (1847–1931), to the discovery of the electron and methods of creating and controlling electron beams by Joseph John Thomson (1856–1940) back to the discovery of primary colors and the rare earth phosphors that make the displays possible. A flat tire can be linked back to the manufacturing technology and discovery of rubber trees that came together precisely in time and place with the nail that is linked back to metallurgy and the creation of iron deposits on earth to the creation of the earth.

Critics of this view claim that all correlations are not causes, but modern experiments in quantum mechanics disclosed that changes in subatomic particles affect others even at some distance apart. So it appears that causation does not always depend upon correlations. If any event in the chain were different, the outcome would be different. As such, even a flat tire is an act of God when you think about it. Dr. Marsha Linehan, originator of dialectical behavior therapy, thought about it and concluded everything that happens is inevitable. Baruch Spinoza (1632–1677) wrote, "In the mind there is no absolute or free will; but the mind is determined to wish this or that by a cause, which has also been determined by another cause, and this last by another cause, and so on to infinity."

With this belief, you can avoid all remorse and guilt, praise and blame for events in the past you wish were different because if they could have been different, they would have been. When he was asked why he writes horror novels, Stephen King replied, "Why do you assume I have a choice? I cannot imagine doing anything else." Whatever happens seems to be the inevitable culmination of untold events one linked upon another. Current events are links in a chain leading into the inevitable future, called casual determinism. And all the links are caused by God. So what appears to be free will actually may be an illusion, necessary is it may be to justify punishing people who break the laws. But there is a catch. St. Clement wrote, "God rules with two hands, Christ in one and Satan in the other." If we are created in the "image and likeness of God" as the Bible says, then are we not all composed of both a Jesus and a devil? And the one that wins is the one he chooses. Recall that Jesus performed exorcisms on people who were demon possessed to show his power, all in the will of God, of course. In scripture, as in life, there does not seem to be any one-sided coins. Belief in both God and Satan must be necessary.

The God that creates the beauty in nature and the infinite cosmos also creates the carnivores who kill and eat each other for food and the cosmic black holes that consume entire galaxies, plus the saints and criminals. God creates drugs for medicine and drugs for addictions, and he makes people susceptible to both. God creates peacemakers and warmongers, diseases and cures. In modern terms, cybersecurity experts who created the Internet and the World Wide Web are balanced with cybersecurity criminals who use it for nefarious purposes. God never made any one-sided coins. If God causes it all, only God can change it. Swiss psychiatrist, C. G. Jung (1875-1961) said, "Man's suffering does not derive from his sins but from the maker of his imperfections, the paradoxical God." Recall the Bible says, "I make peace and create evil/calamity. I, the Lord, do all these things" (Isaiah 45:7). He seems to be indifferent to the consequences of his own creation. Can you believe that?

Here we have an explanation of why Adam and Eve got off on the wrong foot. God made them do it. They did not disobey intentionally. God put the serpent up to tempting them and made them susceptible to temptation. So Jesus petitioned in the "The Lord's Prayer"—"lead us not into temptation" (Matthew 6:13). If God does not tempt people, why bother asking him not to? Perhaps Jesus recalled his temptations by Satan during his sojourn in the wilderness that initiated his ministry, all in God's will, of course. You know, the One who in the beginning created the heavens and the earth and everything in it (Genesis 1:1). Including humankind with the will to disobedience—as any parent with a two-year-old child or rebellious teenagers will attest.

Unfortunately, most people cannot believe that free will is a necessary illusion. We have no free will, so we must believe in free will, and that must be God's will. Scientist, Albert Einstein said man can will what he wants, but he cannot will what he wills. Nothing, from atoms to galaxies, happens outside the will of God, including what we believe. Everyone must necessarily be where they are doing what they are doing instant by instant, or they would be someplace else doing something different. If you can believe that, this work may be very important to your spiritual growth even if you are disabled, live in poverty, or a prison or are driven from your home in a war. With this belief system, you can feel good inside no matter what happens outside—if you work it. If it does not help you feel better inside, perhaps it will help explain why you feel so badly on the outside. In life, pain is inevitable, but suffering is optional. If you still believe the Bible is the Word of God, that must be God's will because it makes no sense otherwise. And of course, you can reject this whole thing and just go outside and play. All in God's will, of course.

Most people adopt the religion they are taught in childhood. Rarely does anyone consider the origin of their belief and research other options. Some people are Mormons, some are Muslims, some are Buddhists, and some are Christians—plus hundreds more religions that are scattered around the world even among indigenous tribes who never heard of the Bible. God makes atheists and agnostics also. C. G. Jung said, "The shoe that fits one pinches another," including all those sitting in churches, synagogues, and mosques, each of whom get something different from the service. Human perception of the benefits in any practice of religion has been studied extensively for centuries with no generally accepted conclusions. The scientific method does not seem to work well in researching religious experience.

Studies show that the practice of any religion can have positive, neutral, and negative effects in the lives, health, and stress of the faithful. Prayer—personal, intercessory, and distant—produces a wide range of results in various situations. The idea that your brain can convince your body a fake treatment is the real thing—the so-called placebo effect—and thus stimulate healing has been around for centuries. Tests of new drugs usually compare results with a benign substance assumed to have no effect, and often, the drug produces little more benefit than the placebo but with significant negative side effects. Faith and belief sometimes seem to cause physical results, but the mechanism between mind and body still has not been established, even in hypnotism—such as that practiced by some faith healers. Sick people may feel better temporarily, but they still die.

Sabeeha Rehman, a Muslim woman, wrote about her respect for different religions: "Five times a day, I am touch with the cosmos at daybreak, noon, afternoon, sunset and nightfall. Every year, I must give 2.5% of my savings to charity, to share God's blessings with those less fortunate.

The ability to let go of money is priceless. Once a year, I fast during the month of Ramadan — from daybreak to sunset, no eating, no drinking (not even water), and no sex. Fasting is an annual refresher course in cultivating restraint, and makes me realize what it is like to go without food. And it makes me God-conscious. Plus, I get an added bonus. I lose weight.

Whenever I begin a task, as in eating a meal or starting the car, I say *"Bismllah."* It means, *I begin in the name of God.* It reminds that we are in God's hands and are asking for His blessings. When I make the intention to do something, as in "see you tomorrow," I add *InshAllah*, meaning God willing. See you tomorrow, *InshAllah*. It's a reminder that man proposes — in this case, woman — and God disposes. If I fail to show up, I can shift the blame to God. It was God's will. (Just kidding!)

What gifts do I admire in other faiths? In the Christian faith, I have always loved the practice of saying Grace at the dinner table, holding hands around the table, and thanking God for the blessing of food. We Muslims should make this a regular practice in *our* daily lives. And of course, I love the spirit of Christmas, Santa Claus ringing the bell for charity, the sparkling Christmas tree, the city as decked out as a Pakistani bride, and all the joy it brings into homes. In the Jewish faith, I believe it is such a sensible idea that one day a week you just rest. Rest, reflect, reset and recharge. I tried it once. I had come back from a Sabbath service, and was so motivated that I decided to observe the Sabbath. It was hard! I kept reaching for my cell phone.

I also believe that the practice of completing the reading of a portion of Torah every week over the course of a year keeps the faith alive. Muslims do that during Ramadan, and then we put away the Quran for the rest of the year, for the most part. Why not make it a weekly thing like the Jews do? In the Hindu faith, I love the music of

> the temples. For centuries, Muslims have fended off music, considering it a distraction at minimum, and lewd at worse. I see no rationale in denying one the joy of the sound of music. Let it in and let it stir your soul, and feel your heart thump with a happy beat. Then of course, there is yoga, which is on my bucket list.
>
> In Buddhism, I treasure the gift of meditation. The cure for all stresses, anxieties, tensions and fears, and an alternative to anti-depressants and tranquilizers. Imagine starting your day with clearing your head, and ending the day by instilling quiet. We could all use that. (www.sabeeharehman.com)

Moreover, some people change their minds with new information, and some don't. Some people reach a plateau in life and stay there, and some continue growing until they die. The late world-famous cellist Pablo Casals continued to practice several hours each day into his eighties because he said, "I think I am still making progress." All in God's will, of course, as there can be no other. That may sound too simplistic, but it is the only plausible answer after you strip away all the futile attempts to find a better explanation for what happens in the world. In fact, it is the ultimate answer to the ubiquitous "why" question—God's will because that reply includes everything in the universe from atoms to galaxies.

The church of my youth and the tradition of my family could not contain the growth that comes with openness to all the religions of the world. I had to develop a belief system that accommodated the world as it is. I learned there is no benefit in judging anyone who follows a different pathway, and no one can take the walk for another. C. G. Jung said, "Your pathway is not my pathway. Therefore, I cannot teach you. The pathway is within." If it is all God's will, then you can feel good inside no matter what happens outside because Jesus said, "The spirit gives life, the flesh counts for nothing. The words I have given you are full of spirit (aka energy) and of life" (John 6:63). He also said before you criticize the speck of sawdust in the eye of another to remove the plank in your own vision (Matthew 7:3). For those with faith, no proof is necessary; and for those without faith, no proof is sufficient. All in God's will, of course.

Faith and reason seem to be mutually exclusive sides of human nature, and faith trumps reason in the religious experience. American theologian William James described religious experience thus: "No adequate report of its contents can be given in words. Its quality must be directly experienced; it cannot be imparted or transferred to others. They are more like states of feeling than like states of intellect. No one can make clear to another who has never had such a feeling, in what the quality or worth of it consists. and something in you absolutely knows the result must be truer than any logic-chopping rationalistic talk, however clever, that may contradict it. They are states of insight into depths of truth unplumbed by the discursive intellect. They are illuminations, revelations, full of significance and importance, all inarticulate though they remain; and as a rule, they carry with them a curious sense of authority for after-time" (*The Variety of Religious Experience*, 1902, 2016). This experience may be unique for each person and totally unsolicited, but perhaps it can be explained in general by reference to the theory of personality described in the Myers-Briggs Type Indicator presented in appendix D.

A New Revelation

The untimely death of my wife at her age of fifty-two thrust me into a deep grief that I never anticipated. I had to find an answer to the ubiquitous question, "Why?" My knowledge of the Bible and my roles as a deacon and Sunday school teacher were no comfort. I feared for my survival, and I hated God for his willy-nilly habit of killing people with war, disease, natural disasters, crimes, etc. Swiss psychiatrist, C. G. Jung said his suffering mental patients got sick because they lost whatever was provided by their religion and were not cured until they got it back. So, I began a deep search for a new spiritual belief that would accommodate the world as it is. After two decades of research into many beliefs, meditation, and therapy, I found my solution or rather it found me. I call it belief in theofatalism, (a.k.a. theological determinism.) This belief came to me through discovery of the Hindu worship of the Trimurti composed of three Gods,

Brahma, Shiva, and Vishnu, the Gods of creation, maintenance, and destruction. They appeared to me as a unitary trinity of Generator, Operator, Destroyer, that is GOD, not to be confused with God in the Bible.

This trinity seems to be a more practical and realistic depiction of reality than the inferred trinity in the Bible. This is not a three-fold God that looks and acts like people he created in his own image. I see it as the prime force in the universe that controls everything from atoms to galaxies—Generator, Operator, Destroyer—as three in one. This is the GOD above Gods in all the man-made religions that creates those religions. Nothing seems to happen outside the will of this GOD, including the scriptures about God in the Bible and worship of the gods in all the other religions of the world. This belief also would have to include the arguments for and against belief in theofatalism. With this belief, you may be able to feel good inside no matter what happens outside. Perhaps like Job, who lost his wealth, family, and his health, we could say, "The Lord gives and takes away—praise to the Lord." (Job 1:21)

Unfortunately, our society values happiness and success as essential goals and focuses on the material world while devaluing the immaterial spiritual world. Moreover, Christians claim that God does not cause suffering, which originated in the original sin of mankind. (Zephaniah 1:17, Romans 3:23) Things do not work out as planned, people disappoint, and all beginnings come with endings. The good suffer and the bad prosper. Perhaps we are given problems to learn how to solve problems. There are only three options: (1) God wants to prevent suffering, but he cannot; (2) God could prevent suffering, but he chooses not to; or (3) God is the one causing the suffering. Theofatalism concludes that the latter is the most logical option, based on the evidence. This belief likely is troublesome for many Christians to consider, much less accept. If you fit into this group, please reserve your judgment until you finish reading this discussion.

The evidence for theofatalism is too extensive for this brief discussion, but it will suffice to provide sufficient grist for the argument. I found many resources in fields of science, sociology, anthropology, psychology, philosophy, religion, politics, and economics leading to the inevitable inference of a GOD above all gods. Just as science assumes the existence of undetectable black holes and dark matter in the cosmos by inference from the laws of gravity, so can theofatalism be inferred from logical reasoning. Albert Einstein said, "Human beings, vegetables, or cosmic dust, we all dance to a mysterious tune intoned in the distance by an invisible player." Shakespeare wrote that all the world's a stage and men and women merely are the players, each with their entries and exits. British theologian emeritus, Paul Helm says, "Not only every atom and molecule but also every thought and intention are under the control of GOD." Christians who cherry pick scriptures claim that God gave man freedom to accept or reject his only son as savior. But Jesus said, "No one can come unto me unless the Father causes/enables them." (John 6:44,65) "You should say if it is the Lord's will we will live and do this or that." (James 4:13-16) I bet you don't get that in church.

Christians often say, "God is in control" without thinking much about what that really means. If we can assume that all thoughts and behaviors come from GOD, then a lot of the suffering and insanity—maybe all of it—in the world begins to make sense. This view of GOD as Generator, Operator, Destroyer permits all the pieces of the puzzle of life on earth in its many forms—plant, animal and human—to fit together. The Bible affirms this belief in scriptures you are not likely to get in church as follows: "The Lord kills and makes alive; The Lord makes poor and makes rich; He brings some low and lifts some up." (1 Samuel 2:6–7) "I make peace and create evil/calamity." (Isaiah 45:7) In this context, the Hebrew word for "evil" is translated elsewhere in the Bible as, spoiled, bad, adversity, trouble, sinful, misfortune, calamity, so take your pick. "When a disaster comes to a city, has not the Lord caused it?" (Amos 3:6) "Though you build your nest as high as the eagle's, from there I will bring you down, declares the Lord." (Jeremiah 49:16, Obadiah 1:4) "Who has spoken and it came to pass, unless the Lord has commanded it? Is it not from the mouth of the most high God that good and bad come?" (Lamentations 3:37-38) "When times are good, be happy; but when times are bad, consider this: God has made the one as well as the other." (Ecclesiastes 7:14) The Quran says the same thing to Muslims; "No calamity comes, no affliction occurs, except by the decision and preordainment of Allah." (S:64.11)

It follows that the only reasonable answer to the ubiquitous question—why?—is it must be GOD's will, or it would be different. This assumption would include beliefs of atheists and agnostics, as well as the religious, because GOD makes them all. After all the man-made holy books, including the Bible, are found to be impotent and flawed, this belief can provide some firm ground on which to stand. Theofatalism has all the generation, operation, and destruction—everything that happens in the universe—covered, from atoms to galaxies, in my opinion.

Theofatalism comes with five principles: (1) everything must be necessary or it would be different, including all the many different belief systems; (2) people make decisions subconsciously they do not control while assuming the expected benefits are more valuable than the burdens, including their beliefs in unprovable religions; (3) the universe is composed of necessary opposites, as in the ancient Chinese symbols of yin and yang, which includes the good and evil in each person; (4) the future is indefinitely uncertain, including what happens after death, and; (5) GOD – Generator, Operator, Destroyer - is everywhere in everything from atoms to galaxies as immaculate immanence.

It follows from the above principles of theofatalism that to be content, which is the Buddhist solution to suffering, one must follow five steps in ADTDA thinking: (1) *Accept* what is moment by moment because it must be necessary or it would be different; (2) *Detach* from what you cannot change and wish was different because it hurts too much not to; (3) *Transcend* the need for control because in reality you don't have any as the brain has a mind of its own; (4) *Don't fight* with GOD, because you cannot win. You must walk the labyrinth pathway you are given, and (5) *Assume* there are no mistakes, only choices and consequences—All in GOD's will of course.

Theofatalism accommodates both acceptance and rejection of this reasoning as well as adoption of other belief systems. Everything must have its complementary opposite because GOD never made any one-sided coins, such as up and down, in and out, sweet and sour, good and evil, male and female, anima and animus, cold and hot, pessimism and optimism, active and passive, content and discontent, creation and destruction, predator and prey, criminal and victim, love and hate, joy and suffering, sickness and health, rich and poor, pain and pleasure, positive and negative, light and dark, truth and falsity, first and last, win and lose, war and peace, birth and death, maze and labyrinth, random and destined, insignificant and indispensable, heaven and hell, Christ and Satan. Knowledge and wisdom also have their opposites. King Solomon wrote that much wisdom brings much sorrow and much knowledge brings much grief. (Ecclesiastes 1:18) Anything apart from its opposite is meaningless. The opposites are required to make the whole. F. Scott Fitzgerald said, "It is a mark of maturity to hold the opposites and still function normally."

> Swiss psychiatrist, C.G. Jung said there is the thing/idea and the symbol of the thing. This new revelation has a symbol of its own. The symbol in Catholic churches is the crucifix and in protestant churches it is the empty cross. The symbol of theofatalism depicted on the cover of this book is the ancient labyrinth inlaid in the cathedral of Chartres, France (1200 CE) where there is only one pathway for each one to follow. After we emerge from the center at birth, we go out into the world following the pathway we are given through stages of infancy, childhood, youth and adulthood. After we pass midlife, we go back again through stages of maturity, seniority, contemplation and mortality to the origin of life. The body returns to basic elements of the earth, but the energy of life can neither be created or destroyed. Unlike the dead ends and random pathway of a maze, which are intentionally designed to confuse and to frustrate, the labyrinth has no barriers, and it definitely is not a random walk.
>
> The Reverend Lauren Artress wrote, "Walking the labyrinth has reemerged today as a metaphor for the spiritual journey and a powerful tool for transformation. This walking meditation is an archetype, a mystical ritual found in many religious traditions. It quiets the mind and opens the soul. Each step unites faith and action as trav-

> elers take one step at a time, living each moment in trust and willingness to follow the course set before them." *(Walking a Labyrinth,* 2011) Labyrinths in several sizes are available for sale. I keep one at my dining table and finger-walk through it after each meal. Visit www.bwatsonstudios.com.

Buddhist nun, Pema Chodran wrote, "The spiritual journey involves going beyond hope and fear, stepping into unknown territory, continually moving forward. The most important aspect of being on the spiritual pathway may be to just keep on moving." (*When Things Fall Apart,* 2016) And it all must be GOD's will, or it would be different. The Bible says, "It is God who directs the lives of his creatures; everyone's life is in his power." (Job 12:10, GNT) It seems like this applied to Jesus also when he prayed, "My Father, if it is possible, may this cup be taken from me. Yet not as I will, but as you will." (Matthew 26:39) If you need more scriptures consider this: "Go to now, you that say, today or tomorrow we will go into such a city, and continue there a year, and buy and sell, and make money: Whereas you know not what shall be on the morrow. For what is your life? It is even a vapor, which appears for a little time, and then vanishes away. Therefore, you ought to say, if the Lord wills, we shall live and do this or that." (James 4:13–15). If it is true, this belief must apply to everyone, everywhere, all the time, including those who believe in free will and those who don't. Gravity does not ask for your permission, and neither does GOD.

Perhaps this belief in theofatalism will be confirmed at some future time, or maybe not. Every great new idea that challenges establishments must survive attacks and rejection before it is accepted. The existence of atoms was just a theory until they became visible through a miraculous electron microscope. The law of gravity was not confirmed until nearly eighty years after it was proposed by Sir Isaac Newton. Classical artist, Vincent van Gogh committed suicide when he could not sell his paintings, but now they sell for millions of dollars. Although it is impeccably logical, theofatalism may need to run the gauntlet of trial before it is acknowledged.

Critics of theofatalism may pose two arguments. One lies in its apparent negation of conscious free will, which people seem to need to believe. They say if we have no free will, then hope for improving our lives disappears under a blanket of depression and despair. Assumption of free will is the international basis for jurisprudence because without it there would be no justification for laws or their enforcement. Apostle Paul wrote, "Let everyone be subject to the governing authorities, for there is no authority except that which God has established. Consequently, whoever rebels against the authority is rebelling against what God has instituted, and those who do so will bring judgment on themselves." (Romans 13: 1-7) If Ralph Waldo Emerson was correct, and we all have within us the capacity for every crime, what separates the criminal from the saint? How come some people yield to temptation while others do not, if not from free will? Without assumed free will, all actions would be robotic, and people could not be held responsible for the results of their uncontrollable impulses. However, if, as in Christianity, people are born sinners destined for hell without a redeeming savior, where is the free will?

Proponents of free will also may argue that scripture claims free will is a gift from God as it lets people love and obey him because they choose to do so. (Matthew 22: 37, John 3: 16, 14: 15). However, free will is negated in other scriptures because there must be necessary opposites. The Jews who rejected Jesus did so because that was their destiny. (Isaiah 6:9–10, Matthew 10:13–15, Mark 4:10–12, 1 Peter 2:8) Apostle Paul wrote that about everyone: " For God has bound everyone over to disobedience so that he may have mercy on them all." (Roman 11: 32) King David proclaimed his life was predestined. "You saw me before I was born and scheduled each day of my life before I began to breathe." (Psalm 139:16)

Another criticism of theofatalism involves possibly confusing correlation with causation. Critics of theofatalism may claim that just because two events are related does not prove they are causative. The theory of causal determinism says all events are inevitable because they are caused by previous events in a chain linking back to the First Cause. Drug addicts exist because GOD created the plants that produce drugs and the people with ability to be addicted and then brought the two together. A flat tire happened because rubber was discovered and processed into tires, and nails come from iron that is mixed with tin to make steel that is used to make nails and they must arrive at the same place at the same time. Our thoughts also are less free than we think. Baruch Spinoza (1632-1677) wrote, "In the mind there is no absolute or free will; the mind is determined to wish this or that by a cause, which has also been determined by another cause, and this last by another cause, and so on to infinity." Events occurring now are links in the chain of unknowable events in the inevitable future. All in GOD's will of course.

Common sense would say people can do things differently than they do, but no one—neither saint or sinner—can go back in time to do anything differently. If anything in the past should have been different it would have been. There is no place in theofatalism for remorse and regrets because there are no mistakes, only inevitable choices and consequences. Humans are very adaptable as indicated by those who cannot live without their cell phones and those who live in primitive tribes as hunter-gatherers. Everyone is where they must be, doing what they must be doing, including those living in mansions, prisons, hospitals, and refugee camps. If not, they would be someplace else doing something different. You don't have to search for your purpose in life because you cannot avoid it.

Theofatalism acknowledges the opposing views of free will and causal determinism as necessary opposites in the same way that God is perceived in the Bible both as love and a raging fire. (1 John 4: 8, Hebrews 10:27) Theofatalism postulates that whatever people believe or eventually discover is the consequence of the will of GOD. Whether you agree or disagree also must be the will of GOD. Mystical writer Abd-ru-shin (aka Oskar Bernhardt), who was big on free will, intuition, and personal volition declared in *The Grail Message* (1941). "All teachings were at one time willed by God, precisely adapted to the individual peoples and countries, and formed in complete accord with their actual spiritual maturity and receptivity." Various people are Catholics, Protestants, Buddhists, Hindus, atheists, republicans and democrats. Thus, belief in theofatalism removes intolerance from all beliefs.

Albert Einstein said, "Man can will what he wants, but he cannot will what he wills. The answer comes to you and you don't know how or why." I conclude that nothing happens outside the will of GOD, including the acceptance and rejection of theofatalism. So, if you agree or disagree with this conclusion, never fear, because I think that GOD is creating your thoughts as well as your actions.

> The human body comprises matter and energy. At any given moment, roughly 20 watts of energy course through your body — enough to power a dim light bulb. Mostly, we get it through the consumption of food, which is transformed into chemical energy. That chemical energy is then transformed into kinetic energy that is ultimately used to power our muscles. The same can be said about plants, which are powered by photosynthesis, a process that allows them to transform energy from sunlight into growth.
>
> In death, the collection of atoms in the elements of which your body is composed are recycled back into the universe from which they came. Since, according to the law of universal conservation, energy can neither be created nor destroyed, it follows that death of the body does not extinguish its energetic existence. Whether the body is cremated or interred, the essence of your energy and its related field— not to be confused with your biological consciousness — will continue to exist throughout space until the end of time. Your existence merely changes from one form of energy into another, i.e., from physical to spiritual. If the science is true, survivors may be comforted to know your energy is still around; you are just reborn and, possibly, waiting to be recycled. To Christians, Jesus said you must be born again in spirit to enter the kingdom of Heaven. (John 3:3) (Wikipedia)

To learn more about theofatalism, refer to my books titled *Voices of Sedona, Baby Boomer Lamentations, Theofatalism, and A Labyrinth Walk of Life, Creating Serenity in Chaos, Better Living Better Dying*, and *My Resurrection from Hell—A Christian Widower's Story*. If this new revelation resonates with you, perhaps you can organize a discussion group to keep it going. Perhaps someone will accept a call to carry this message forward to all those who need it, as did the Apostle Paul with the message of Jesus.

Final Steps

Those who depend upon Bible scriptures to define the way to happiness and contentment may discover more confusion than clarity. Jesus told those disciples who believed in him, "If you hold to my teaching, you are really my disciples. Then you will know the truth, and the truth will set you free" (John 8:32). However, when Pilate asked him, "What is truth?" Jesus remained silent. (John 18:28) Of course, it does not matter what people think about it, does it? Truth is truth whether we believe it or not. Knowledge, or lack of it, doesn't matter either. The law of gravity existed for millennia before Sir Isaac Newton discovered it. So did all the laws of physics and chemistry exist before they were discovered. I have learned from extensive searches that the ocean of knowledge never is full because there always is more to learn, and new truth emerges with new discoveries, sometimes voiding previous knowledge. People all must absorb new information and adapt to changing times in order to thrive. But this process of adaptation has its limits, and eventually, time takes its toll. Like Dr. Jung said at the end of his long career, we might say, "I confess I am afraid of a long-drawn-out suffering. It seems to me as if I am ready to die, although as it looks to me some powerful thoughts are still flickering like lightnings in a summer night. Yet they are not mine, they belong to God, as everything else which bears mentioning." After he had a heart attack and reported a near-death experience, Jung said, "I do not have to believe because I know." Others who report near-death experiences also describe a real awareness of an afterlife. Such a spiritual experience may not be captured by the intellect. Still, to be useful, any belief system must make sense in every circumstance and be subject to revision with new information.

A successful life requires everyone to be true to themselves, wherever it leads. Bertrand Russell (1872–1970) wrote, "What makes a freethinker is not his beliefs but the way in which he holds them.

If he holds them because his elders told him they were true when he was young, or if he holds them because if he did not he would be unhappy, his thought is not free; but if he holds them because, after careful thought he finds a balance of evidence in their favor, then his thought is free, however odd his conclusions may seem." Freedom to believe where reason takes you is balanced with what makes you feel good about life and death. When reason and emotion are focused on the same belief, there lies the truth for you.

The late anthropologist Margaret Mead observed as a culture, when a baby is born we rejoice, when a couple marries we celebrate, but when someone dies, we pretend nothing happened. It is stressful to focus on the truth like every day, every hour, every minute is one more and one less of your life. Professor of psychiatry emeritus Irvin Yalom described contemplating our own mortality as "staring at the sun" because it can only be viewed in small short glimpses. You can run, but you cannot hide. In the end we all must die and give up the identity we spent our whole life building to leave behind everything and everyone we love. The worst thing about dying may be realizing life is going on without you. Everyone dies, and nobody knows what happens next. In the United States, about 2,600,000 people die each year; 7,100 each day; and 296 each hour. Unless it affects your house, death is not part of the normal life experience. The body seems to be a temporary vessel that permits the spirit to have a human experience. The great king David wrote, "Our days may come to seventy years, or eighty, if our strength endures; yet the best of them are but trouble and sorrow, for they quickly pass, and we fly away" (Psalm 90:10). Jesus said God is God of the living and not of the dead and the dead should bury their own dead, so perhaps there is some scripture support for our social taboo about dying (Matthew 8:22, Mark 12:27).

The young may die and the old must die. Eventually something fails that cannot be treated. Half of all Americans die by age eighty and most of the rest by age ninety. For many of us, the last few years can be very unpleasant. The late Steve Jobs, founder of Apple Inc. who died at age fifty-seven, said he noticed that even those who think they are going to heaven don't want to die to get there. The late senator John McCain observed that although people all know that no one lives forever, everyone hopes they might be an exception. Don't bet on it. In my opinion, dying is not something that happens to us, it is something we do when the time is right. It may be more painful for survivors than for the deceased. When facing his demise, the late actor Charlton Heston declared, "I must reconcile equal measures of courage and surrender." The late religious skeptic Christopher Hitchens lamented that the hardest thing about dying is realizing that the party is going without you.

The late psychiatrist Elizabeth Kubler-Ross observed that people facing death proceed through stages of shock, denial, anger, bargaining, and depression before they come to accept their fate (*On Death and Dying,* 1969). I suffered all of them watching my wife die, and still I do not fully accept my own mortality. After losing thirty-three loved ones, coworkers, and neighbors, I conclude dying is easy, trying not to is hard, often humiliating and painful, and usually very expensive. Surviving loss of a beloved spouse is rated the highest in stress caused by life changes.

Although I grieved the losses immensely, I was glad their suffering ended and the spirits were released from their worn-out bodies. Plus, my losses motivated me to research and write a book on grieving with a cowriter who is a psychologist and a seminary professor. In it, we discussed five tasks of grief: acknowledge the loss, feel the feelings, find healthy substitutes, detach from investments in the past, and continue on your pathway of life. If interested, read my book titled *Recovery from Loss.* Grieving our losses seems to be a necessary response that Jesus recognized, "Blessed are those who mourn for they will be comforted." (Matthew 5:4) He did not explain how. In fact, he told one mourning disciple who asked for permission to go home and bury his father, "Follow me and let the dead bury their own dead." (Matthew 8:22) How are we to interpret this scripture? It seems that grief is felt in proportion to the emotional investment one makes in the object. If the loss is permanent, grief and its related depression may be present for the remainder of life to some extent as the new normal.

Medical systems are organized to keep people alive as long as possible without consideration of the quality of life. Many people are unaware of their medical options and are deprived of personal control even when it is possible at the end of life. Everyone should have access to compassionate choices including palliative care, which are coordinated medical, physical, social, and spiritual comfort; hospice care, which is pain management with physical comfort; and physician-aided termination if desired when life expectancy is less than six months. The latter is legalized in California, Oregon, Washington, Montana, Vermont, and the District of Columbia and in some countries; but more debate is needed about this option. Society is evolving slowly, one state at a time.

Doctors are bound to continue treatment unless restrained by some intervention. The medical model of treatment with patented synthesized drugs, radiation, and surgery in America is driven more by profit than efficacy. Perhaps the research into medical physics will produce some better treatment options in a post-biological world. Also, gene editing has been demonstrated as a new treatment for DNA related disabilities. The phenomenon of placebo effect often is as good as the treatment, except possibly for orthopedics. Jesus healed by faith and prayer, and some people are skeptical of common insurance-driven treatments. Perhaps the mind does rule the body, as the late Mary Baker Eddy promoted. A severe emotional shock such as a terminal diagnosis can impact the brain in ways that limit its recovery. However, you can reject treatment if the legal requirements are met. A patient is the doctor's customer and not a slave. At a minimum, everyone should discuss their treatment wishes with family, prepare a legal living will or medical directive specifying your wishes for treatment, and designate someone as medical proxy to control treatment when you cannot do so. More education and government actions are required for people to obtain better control of their own dying. Such progress requires a measure of faith, dedication, and resilience, all in GOD's will, of course.

Unfortunately, some people are given more burdens than they can carry. For some people, death is not the worst thing in life and suicide is a reasonable exit. Celebrity chef, Anthony Bourdain and actor, Robin Williams both chose that option. The enemy is not death, but uncontrollable suffering, and people have varying degrees of tolerance. Jesus told his disciple: "Very truly I tell you, when you were younger you dressed yourself and went where you wanted; but when you are old you will stretch out your hands, and someone else will dress you and lead you where you do not want to go" (John 21:18). The bane of old age is losing control of your life style. Fear and anger are appropriate reactions. Everyone deserves the right to die on their own terms when the time is right for them. For more information on healthy living and terminal life planning, visit www.finalexitnetwork.org and read my book titled *Better Living, Better Dying*.

The truth is life is not fair, some of the good people suffer and some of the bad prosper, people disappoint us, plans do not work out, all beginnings come with endings, and everyone leaves their body to return it to the stellar dust from which it came, and nobody knows what comes after. Everyone must pass through the riddle of death without knowing where they are going after they die – scriptures notwithstanding. We live in a world of volatility, uncertainty, complexity, and ambiguity while trying to hang onto what we are taught will make us happy in our specific cultures. Dr. Jung said all of his disturbed patients had lost the support that religious faith provided, and none of them got well without regaining it—what he called making peace with God. He used the word "god" to refer to the mysterious powers of the universe: "God is the name by which I designate all things which cross my path violently and recklessly, all things which upset my subjective views, plans and intentions, and change the course of my life for better or for worse." Perhaps Jung would accept this concept of God in scriptures: "[God] is over all and through all and in all" and "from [God] and through him and to him are all things" (Ephesians 4:6, Romans 11:36). Discerning readers may find here a hint and possible forecast of panentheism, which is principle 5 in theofatalism.

This is not a god to be worshipped or loved, but rather one to be feared, or maybe both as one would respond to a father figure who both provides and disciplines. "Fear him who, after your body has been killed, has authority to throw you into hell. Yes, I say, fear him" (Luke 12:5). "You do not delight in sacrifice, or I would bring it; you do not take pleasure in burnt offerings. My sacrifice, O God, is a broken spirit; a broken and contrite heart you, God, will not despise" (Psalm 51:16–18). I know that everything God does will endure forever; nothing can be added to it and nothing taken from it. God does it so that people will fear him." (Ecclesiastes 3:14)

The late Helen Schuman, scribe of *A Course in Miracles* (1975), wrote, "Disobeying God is meaningful only to the insane; in truth it is impossible." As it is with individuals, so it is with nations and cultures, which are composed of individuals. If GOD is in control of everything, agnostics, atheists, and the LGBT community will find comfort in theofatalism because GOD made them too. Consider the sexual transition of Bruce Jenner, 1976 Olympic Decathlon champion and father of three sons and three daughters from three marriages, to transgender Caitlin Jenner at the age of sixty-five. C. G. Jung detected that both sexes contain elements of the other (anima in men and animus in women) that is repressed/denied for fear the opposite will take over. Sometimes they are right—especially as they get older. But everyone is a member of the human community that GOD created, and no one can resign or be expelled.

The creation has no power to criticize the Creator. We are the clay and it is the potter making some for common use and some for royal use (Jeremiah 18:2–6, Romans 9:12). "Each person should live as a believer in whatever situation the Lord has assigned to them, just as God has called them" (1 Corinthians 7:20). Get it? Saint/Mother Teresa (1910–1997) concluded, "God does whatever he wants with whomever he wants, and we all must take what he gives and give what he takes…with a smile." So if you don't get it, that must be the will of GOD as there can be no other, which may be the most important piece of wisdom that you can possibly learn, but the benefits come with burdens, as usual. The road to enlightenment can be a lonely struggle, and there may be no light at the end of the tunnel, or maybe no end to the tunnel, or maybe no tunnel. Someone said, "Before enlightenment I chopped wood and carried water, and after enlightenment I chopped wood and carried water."

Unfortunately, enlightenment has its price. Great king Solomon learned that with much wisdom comes much sorrow and the more knowledge the more grief (Ecclesiastes 1:18). After his own discoveries about the human psyche, Dr. Jung was borderline despondent: "I suffer from the fact that I can so seldom have a conversation with an adequate partner. I have suffered enough from incomprehension and from the isolation one falls into when one says things that people do not understand." I also have felt such isolation in trying to get even a few people to understand the concept of theofatalism. I often wonder if my writing merely is a journaling to myself. I am a man on the riverbank yelling at people floating by having a party on a houseboat while they are heading for a waterfall. But even if they heard me, it would not change anything because we all must play the roles we are assigned and walk the pathway we are given. As with the law of gravity, life is what it is for each person, and I have concluded it must be necessary as it is, or it would be different. Famous classical painter, Vincent van Gogh committed suicide at his age thirty-seven depressed and impoverished because people would not buy his paintings – now they are worth many millions. If he had survived, perhaps he might have lived to be rich and famous, but it was not to be. Ergo theofatalism.

Very few people can handle the truth, especially the truth about the Bible, because the world of imagination and proof texting feels much safer, so please feel especially gifted if you are reading this. If you don't get it, that doesn't matter. The perceived truth is all relative to time and place and is likely to change depending on the pathway you are given. Poet Robert Frost (1874–1963) wrote, "I took the road less traveled, and it made all the difference." People lived under the law of gravity without knowing it before Isaac Newton proposed it in 1687, and it was not confirmed until 1798, seventy-one years after his death. It may be that way with theofatalism, or not. St. Thomas à Kempis wrote in *The Imitation of Christ* (1427), "It is better to leave everyone to their own way of thinking rather than give way to contentious discourse." Mystical writer Abd-ru-shin (a.k.a. Oskar Bernhardt (1875–1941) who was big on free will, intuition, and personal volition declared in *The Grail Message* (1941):

"All (religious) teachings/thoughts/ideas/interpretations were at one time willed by God, precisely adapted to the individual peoples and countries, and formed in complete accord with their actual spiritual maturity and receptivity."

There is no need to search for your purpose in life because you cannot avoid it. Theofatalism says you are right where you are supposed to be doing what you are doing and thinking what you are thinking. By this measure, everyone is successful, including those living in prisons and refugee camps as well as mansions. This conclusion may be difficult to accept if you live in prison or a refugee camp, but there does not seem to be any exceptions. In the great scheme of things, we all seem to be insignificant but indispensable like a grain of sand on the beach or a drop of water in the ocean or a single fish in the sea. Even those few called to momentary greatness disappear into the sands of history. When he was facing the Cuban missile crisis in October 1962, President John F. Kennedy said, "I see a storm coming and if God has a place for me in it, I think I am ready." A year later, he was assassinated. The earth is a small blue dot in the vastness of space surrounded by billions and billions of other dots of light in the universe. Maybe it all comes down to the conclusion that since we cannot change what we are or are becoming, the only salvation for humanity is to turn ourselves over to the Creator because, as the song says, "He's got the whole world in his hands." Some do, and some don't, all in GOD's will, of course, ergo theofatalism.

It may be appropriate to include a statement from renowned scientist Albert Einstein, quoted by cosmologist, Carl Sagan: "I cannot conceive of a god who rewards and punishes his creatures or has a will of the kind we experience in ourselves. Neither can I nor would I want to conceive of an individual who survives his physical death; let feeble souls, from fear or absurd egotism, cherish such thoughts. I am satisfied with the mystery of eternity and a glimpse of the marvelous structure of the existing world, together with the devoted striving to comprehend a portion of it, be it ever so tiny, of the Reason that manifests itself in nature" (*Billions and Billions*, 1998, 266). From this perspective, one may choose to look for the Creator in the study of his creation, be it from the smallest atomic particle to the most distant galaxy, including all life-forms on earth, Homo sapiens being only one of them.

Perhaps the end of life can be proclaimed with these words of Apostle Paul: "I am already being poured out like a drink offering, and the time for my departure is near. I have fought the good fight, I have finished the race, I have kept the faith. Now there is in store for me the crown of righteousness, which the Lord, the righteous Judge, will award to me on that day—and not only to me, but also to all who have longed for his appearing. Therefore, we do not lose heart. Though outwardly we are wasting away, yet inwardly we are being renewed day by day… For our light and momentary troubles are achieving for us an eternal glory that far outweighs them all. So we fix our eyes not on what is seen, but on what is unseen, since what is seen is temporary, but what is unseen is eternal. "When the perishable has been clothed with the imperishable, and the mortal with immortality, then the saying that is written will come true: Death has been swallowed up in victory" (Philippians 3:10-14, 1 Corinthians 15:54, 2 Corinthians 4:16-18, 2 Timothy 4:6-8). During his last days, the late Senator John McCain, who was a war prisoner in North Vietnam for seven years said, "I have had a great life. I would not change a thing, and I am so grateful." Perhaps he learned to separate spirit from flesh as Jesus declared, "The spirit gives life, the flesh counts for nothing" (John 6:63). That may be a tall order for us mere humans.

It may be possible to know too much about the Bible. Is it just a book of myths and legends or something more? It seems to fulfill a human need to believe in something immaterial, including belief in myths and legends. It may have been written, copied, and translated countless times during the past two thousand years. It may be flawed, inconsistent, full of contradictions, and badly in need of an editor. Proof texting must be necessary and so must be criticism of proof texting. It seems we need some understanding that would accommodate both sides in the necessary opposites of scriptures and of life. There are no one-sided coins, and theofatalism seems to provide such understanding. I don't know if it is true or not, but I know that whatever you or I think about it will not change the truth. Unfortunately, modern social media has made truth relative to the belief of the recipient—what many people believe, they think is true. Political campaigns illustrate this trend because they often publish more propaganda than facts, so elections are driven more by fake news than truth. But hey, are not all religions based on the same idea? Some things are much bigger than mere human beings, as yet, can understand.

Nevertheless, many people in every generation search the Bible for what it can mean to each one in this life and beyond. So it must be the symbol of something greater than its contents—like the image of Santa Claus symbolizes the joy of Christmas, and the image of the crucified Christ on the cross may symbolize infinite compassion and love, and the labyrinth is the symbol of theofatalism. Dr. Jung said there seems to be a hunger or emptiness in the collective unconscious mind of humankind yearning to be filled by religions and holy books. For many Christians, the answer is in their God and his Son. St. Augustine of Hippo (354–430 CE) wrote, "Our hearts are restless until we rest in you." And Jesus replies, "Here I am! I stand at the door and knock. If anyone hears my voice and opens the door, I will come in and eat with that person, and they with me" (Revelation 3:20). Or you can go to his house, "Ask and it will be given to you; seek and you will find; knock and the door will be opened to you" (Matthew 7:7, Luke 11:9–10). Everyone who reads this must ask themselves, "What has that got to do with me?"

Appendix A

Commandments Of Jesus

(St. Joseph, the World Parish, www.stjw.ca)

OBEY: "If you want to enter life, keep the commandments. Which ones? he inquired. Jesus replied, You shall not murder, you shall not commit adultery, you shall not steal, you shall not give false testimony, honor your father and mother, and love your neighbor as yourself. All these I have kept, the young man said. What do I still lack? Jesus answered, If you want to be perfect, go, sell your possessions and give to the poor, and you will have treasure in heaven. Then come, follow me." (Matthew 19:17)

"If you love me, you will keep my commandments." (John 14:15)

REPENT: "From that time Jesus began to proclaim, Repent, for the kingdom of Heaven has come near." (Matthew 4:17)

REJOICE: "Rejoice and be glad, for your reward is great in Heaven, for in the same way they persecuted the prophets who were before you." (Matthew 5:12)

LET YOUR LIGHT SHINE BEFORE OTHERS BUT GIVE GLORY TO GOD: "In the same way, let your light shine before others, so that they may see your good works and give glory to your Father in Heaven." (Matthew 5:16)

DO YOUR ALMS IN SECRET: "Be careful not to practice your righteousness in front of others to be seen by them. If you do, you will have no reward from your Father in heaven. So, when you give to the needy, do not announce it with trumpets, as the hypocrites do in the synagogues and on the streets, to be honored by others. Truly I tell you, they have received their reward in full." (Matthew 6:1–8, 18)

SETTLE MATTERS QUICKLY WITH YOUR ADVERSARY: "Come to terms quickly with your accuser while you are on the way to court with him, or your accuser may hand you over to the judge, and the judge to the guard, and you will be thrown into prison." (Matthew 5:25)

GET RID OF WHATEVER CAUSES YOU TO SIN: "If your right eye causes you to sin, tear it out and throw it away; it is better for you to lose one of your members than for your whole body to be thrown into hell. And if your right hand causes you to sin, cut it off and throw it away; it is better for you to lose one of your members than for your whole body to go into hell." (Matthew 5:29–30)

KEEP YOUR WORD AND LET YOUR WORDS MATCH WHAT'S IN YOUR HEART: "But I say to you, Do not swear at all, either by Heaven, for it is the throne of God, or by the earth, for it is his footstool, or by Jerusalem, for it is the city of the great King. And do not swear by your head, for you cannot make one hair white or black. Let your word be "Yes, Yes" or "No, No"; anything more than this comes from the evil one." (Matthew 5:34–37)

RETURN GOOD FOR EVIL: "But I tell you, do not resist an evil person. If anyone slaps you on the right cheek, turn to them the other cheek also. And if anyone wants to sue you and take your shirt, hand over your coat as well. If anyone forces you to go one mile, go with them two miles. Give to the one who asks you, and do not turn away from the one who wants to borrow from you." (Matthew 5:38-42)

LOVE YOUR ENEMIES: "You have heard that it was said, you shall love your neighbor and hate your enemy. But I say to you, love your enemies and pray for those who persecute you, so that you may be children of your Father in Heaven; for he makes his sun rise on the evil and on the good, and sends rain on the righteous and on the unrighteous." (Matthew 5:43–45)

BE PERFECT: "Be perfect, therefore, as your Heavenly Father is perfect." (Matthew 5:48)

GIVE TO PLEASE GOD, PRAY TO PLEASE GOD AND FAST TO PLEASE GOD; NOT TO BE SEEN: "Beware of practicing your piety before others in order to be seen by them; for then you have no reward from your Father in Heaven. But when you give to the needy, do not let your left hand know what your right hand is doing, so that your giving may be in secret. Then your Father, who sees what is done in secret, will reward you." (Matthew 6:1–3)

THIS IS HOW YOU SHOULD PRAY: "Pray then in this way: Our Father in Heaven, hallowed be your name. Your kingdom come. Your will be done, on earth as it is in Heaven. Give us this day our daily bread. And forgive us our debts, as we also have forgiven our debtors. And do not bring us to the time of trial, but rescue us from the evil one. For if you forgive others their trespasses, your Heavenly Father will also forgive you; but if you do not forgive others, neither will your Father forgive your trespasses." (Matthew 6:9–15)

LAY UP TREASURES IN HEAVEN: "Do not store up for yourselves treasures on earth, where moth and rust consume and where thieves break in and steal; but store up for yourselves treasures in Heaven, where neither moth nor rust consumes and where thieves do not break in and steal. For where your treasure is, there your heart will be also." (Matthew 6:19–21)

DO NOT WORRY ABOUT YOUR NEEDS: "Therefore I tell you, do not worry about your life, what you will eat or what you will drink, or about your body, what you will wear. Is not life more than food, and the body more than clothing? Look at the birds of the air; they neither sow nor reap nor gather into barns, and yet your Heavenly Father feeds them. Are you not of more value than they?" (Matthew 6:25–26)

PLACE GOD FIRST: "But strive first for the kingdom of God and his righteousness, and all these things will be given to you as well." (Matthew 6:33)

DO NOT WORRY ABOUT TOMORROW: "So do not worry about tomorrow, for tomorrow will bring worries of its own. Today's trouble is enough for today." (Matthew 6:34)

DO NOT JUDGE: "Do not judge, so that you may not be judged. For with the judgment you make you will be judged, and the measure you give will be the measure you get." (Matthew 7:1–2) It is more blessed to give than to receive. (Acts 20:35)

GUARD WHAT IS SACRED: "Do not give what is holy to dogs; and do not throw your pearls before swine, or they will trample them under foot and turn and maul you." (Matthew 7:6)

ASK, SEEK, AND KNOCK: "Ask, and it will be given to you; search, and you will find; knock, and the door will be opened for you." (Matthew 7:7)

DO UNTO OTHERS: "In everything do to others as you would have them do to you; for this is the law and the prophets." (Matthew 7:12)

CHOOSE THE NARROW GATE: "Enter through the narrow gate; for the gate is wide and the road is easy that leads to destruction, and there are many who take it. For the gate is narrow and the road is hard that leads to life, and there are few who find it." (Matthew 7:13–14)

BEWARE FALSE PROPHETS: "Beware of false prophets, who come to you in sheep's clothing but inwardly are ravenous wolves." (Matthew 7:15)
In addition: "Dear friends, do not believe every spirit, but test the spirits to see whether they are from God, because many false prophets have gone out into the world. This is how you can recognize the Spirit of God: Every spirit that acknowledges that Jesus Christ has come in the flesh is from God, but every spirit that does not acknowledge Jesus is not from God. This is the spirit of the antichrist, which you have heard is coming and even now is already in the world." (1 John 4:1–3)

BE AS SHREWD AS SERPENTS AND INNOCENT AS DOVES: "See, I am sending you out like sheep into the midst of wolves; so be wise as serpents and innocent as doves." (Matthew 10:16)

COME TO ME ALL WHO LABOUR AND ARE OVERBURDENED: "Take my yoke upon you, and learn from me; for I am gentle and humble in heart, and you will find rest for your souls." (Matthew 11:29)

HONOR YOUR PARENTS: "For God said, "Honor your father and your mother, so your days on earth may be long." and, "Whoever speaks evil of father or mother must surely die." (Matthew 15:4)

HATE YOUR FAMILY AND YOURSELF: "Anyone who loves their father or mother more than me is not worthy of me; anyone who loves their son or daughter more than me is not worthy of me." (Mark 8:34)
"If anyone comes to me and does not hate father and mother, wife and children, brothers and sisters—yes, even their own life—such a person cannot be my disciple." (Matthew 10:37, Luke 14:26)

DO NOT DESPISE CHILDLIKE BELIEVERS: "Take care that you do not despise one of these little ones; for, I tell you, in Heaven their angels continually see the face of my Father in Heaven." (Matthew 18:10)

SETTLE DISPUTES BETWEEN BEIEVERS IN THIS MANNNER: "If another member of the church sins against you, go and point out the fault when the two of you are alone. If the member listens to you, you have regained that one. But if you are not listened to, take one or two others along with you, so that every word may be confirmed by the evidence of two or three witnesses. If the member refuses to listen to them, tell it to the church; and if the offender refuses to listen even to the church, let such a one be to you as a Gentile and a tax-collector." (Matthew 18:15–17)

OBEY THE COMMANDMENTS: "If you want to enter (eternal) life, keep the commandments. You shall not murder, you shall not commit adultery, you shall not steal, you shall not give false testimony, honor your father and mother and love your neighbor as yourself." (Matthew 19:17–19)

AVOID GETTING DIVORCED: "For this reason a man will leave his father and mother and be united to his wife, and the two will become one flesh. So they are no longer two, but one flesh. Therefore, what God has joined together, let no one separate." (Matthew 19:6, Mark 10:8)

LEAD BY BEING A SERVANT: "Whoever wishes to be great among you must be your servant, and whoever wishes to be first among you must be your slave." (Matthew 20:26–27)

CALL NO MAN FATHER: "But you are not to be called 'Rabbi,' for you have one Teacher, and you are all brothers. And do not call anyone on earth 'father,' for you have one Father, and he is in heaven. Nor are you to be called instructors, for you have one Instructor, the Messiah. The greatest among you will be your servant. For those who exalt themselves will be humbled, and those who humble themselves will be exalted." (Matthew 23: 8–12)

PAY TAXES AND SUPPORT THE CHURCH: "Then he said to them, so give back to Caesar what is Caesar's, and to God what is

God's. When they heard this, they were amazed. So, they left him and went away." (Matthew 22:21–22)

"Woe to you, teachers of the law and Pharisees, you hypocrites! You give a tenth of your spices—mint, dill and cumin. But you have neglected the more important matters of the law—justice, mercy and faithfulness. You should have practiced the latter, without neglecting the former. You blind guides! You strain out a gnat but swallow a camel." (Matthew 23:23)

LOVE THE LORD AND LOVE YOUR NEIGHBOR: "He said to him, You shall love the Lord your God with all your heart, and with all your soul, and with all your mind. This is the greatest and first commandment. And a second is like it: "You shall love your neighbor as yourself." (Matthew 22:37–39)

FEAR HIM: "I tell you, my friends, do not be afraid of those who kill the body and after that can do no more. But I will show you whom you should fear: Fear him who, after your body has been killed, has authority to throw you into hell. Yes, I tell you, fear him… His mercy extends to those who fear him, from generation to generation." (Luke 12:4–5, 1:50)

DO NOT EXALT YOURSELF: "But you are not to be called rabbi, for you have one teacher, and you are all students. And call no one your father on earth, for you have one Father—the one in Heaven. Nor are you to be called instructors, for you have one instructor, the Messiah. The greatest among you will be your servant. All who exalt themselves will be humbled, and all who humble themselves will be exalted." (Matthew 23:8–12)

"Many who are last shall be first and the first shall be last." (Matthew 19:30, 20:16; Mark 10:31; Luke 13:30)

PROVIDE FOR THOSE IN DISTRESS: "Then the king will say to those at his right hand, 'Come, you that are blessed by my Father, inherit the kingdom prepared for you from the foundation of the world; for I was hungry and you gave me food, I was thirsty and you gave me something to drink, I was a stranger and you welcomed me, I was naked and you gave me clothing, I was sick and you took care of me, I was in prison and you visited me.'" (Matthew 25:34–36)

GO AND MAKE DISCIPLES OF ALL NATIONS: "Go therefore and make disciples of all nations, baptizing them in the name of the Father and of the Son and of the Holy Spirit, and teaching them to obey everything that I have commanded you. And remember, (even where two or three are gathered in my name) I am with you always, to the end of the age." (Matthew 18:20, 28:19–20)

DO NOT OPPOSE OTHER CHRISTIAN GROUPS: "John said to him, 'Teacher, we saw someone casting out demons in your name, and we tried to stop him, because he was not following us.' But Jesus said, 'Do not stop him; for no one who does a deed of power in my name will be able soon afterwards to speak evil of me. Whoever is not against us is for us." (Mark 9:38–40)

HAVE COMPLETE FAITH IN **FAITH**: "Jesus answered them, Have faith in God. Truly I tell you, if you say to this mountain, Be taken up and thrown into the sea, and if you do not doubt in your heart, but believe that what you say will come to pass, it will be done for you. So I tell you, whatever you ask for in prayer, believe that you have received it, and it will be yours." (Mark 11:22–24)

FORGIVE: "Whenever you stand praying, forgive, if you have anything against anyone; so that your Father in Heaven may also forgive you your trespasses." (Mark 11:25–6)
"Then Peter came to Jesus and asked, Lord, how many times shall I forgive my brother or sister who sins against me? Up to seven times? Jesus answered, I tell you, not seven times, but seventy-seven times." (Matthew 18:21–22)

BE MERCIFUL: "Be merciful, just as your Father is merciful." (Luke 6:36)
"Do unto others as you would have them do unto you." (Luke 6:31)

JUDGING, GIVING, MEASURING: "Do not judge, and you will not be judged. Do not condemn, and you will not be condemned. Forgive, and you will be forgiven. Give, and it will be given to you. A good measure, pressed down, shaken together and running over, will be poured into your lap. For with the measure you use, it will be measured to you." (Luke 6:37–38)

CLEAN UP YOUR ACT FIRST: "Why do you look at the speck of sawdust in your brother's eye and pay no attention to the plank in your own eye? How can you say to your brother, 'Brother, let me take the speck out of your eye,' when you yourself fail to see the plank in your own eye? You hypocrite, first take the plank out of your eye, and then you will see clearly to remove the speck from your brother's eye." (Luke 6:41–42)

PRACTICE THE WORD: "As for everyone who comes to me and hears my words and puts them into practice, I will show you what they are like. They are like a man building a house, who dug down deep and laid the foundation on rock. When a flood came, the torrent struck that house but could not shake it, because it was well built. But the one who hears my words and does not put them into practice is like a man who built a house on the ground (sand) without a foundation. The moment the torrent struck that house, it collapsed and its destruction was complete." (Luke 6:46–49)

TAKE UP YOUR CROSS: "Then he said to them all, 'If any want to become my followers, let them deny themselves and take up their cross daily and follow me.'" (Luke 9:23)

DO AS THE GOOD SAMARITAN DID: "But a Samaritan, as he traveled, came where the man was; and when he saw him, he took pity on him. He went to him and bandaged his wounds, pouring on oil and wine. Then he put the man on his own donkey, brought him to an inn and took care of him. Jesus said, Go and do likewise." (Luke 10:33–34, 37) (*Samaritans were branches of Judaism living in Samaria not recognized by Orthodox Jews.*)

BE READY FOR THE SECOND COMING: "You also must be ready, for the Son of Man is coming at an unexpected hour." (Luke 12:40)
"What good will it be for someone to gain the whole world, yet forfeit their soul? Or what can anyone give in exchange for their soul?" (Matthew 16:26)

DO THIS IN REMEMBRANCE OF ME: "Then he took a loaf of bread, and when he had given thanks, he broke it and gave it to them, saying, This is my body, which is given for you. Do this in remembrance of me. And he did the same with the cup after supper, saying, This cup that is poured out for you is the new covenant in my blood." (Luke 22:19–20)

YOU MUST BE BORN AGAIN: "Very truly I tell you, no one can enter the kingdom of God unless they are born of water and the Spirit. Do not be astonished that I said to you, you must be born from above... With God, everything is possible." (John 3:5–7)

WASH ONE ANOTHER'S FEET: "So if I, your Lord and Teacher, have washed your feet, you also ought to wash one another's feet." (John 13:14)

REMAIN IN ME AND I WILL REMAIN IN YOU: "Abide in me as I abide in you. Just as the branch cannot bear fruit by itself unless it abides in the vine, neither can you unless you abide in me." (John 15:4)

LOVE ONE ANOTHER AS I HAVE LOVED YOU: "This is my commandment, that you love one another as I have loved you." (John 15:12)

Appendix B

Instructions of Apostle Paul

(www.hope-of-israel.org)

"The word is near you; it is in your mouth and in your heart, that is, the message concerning faith that we proclaim: If you declare with your mouth, Jesus is Lord, and believe in your heart that God raised him from the dead, you will be saved. For it is with your heart that you believe and are justified, and it is with your mouth that you profess your faith and are saved." (Romans 10: 8–10)

"Be very careful, then, how you live—not as unwise but as wise, making the most of every opportunity, because the days are evil. Therefore, do not be foolish, but understand what the Lord's will is. Do not get drunk on wine, which leads to debauchery. Instead, be filled with the Spirit, speaking to one another with psalms, hymns, and songs from the Spirit. Sing and make music from your heart to the Lord, always giving thanks to God the Father for everything, in the name of our Lord Jesus Christ." (Ephesians 5:15–20)

"As Christians, we will never be punished for sin. That was done once for all. "There is now no condemnation for those who are in Christ Jesus." (Romans 8:1, Galatians 5:19–21)

"Not in rioting and drunkenness, not in chambering and wantonness, not in strife and envying, but put on the Lord Jesus Christ, and make no provision for the flesh to fulfill the lusts thereof." (Romans 13:13–14)

"But now I have written unto you not to keep company, if any man that is called a brother be a fornicator, or covetous, or an idolator, or a railer, or a drunkard, or an extortioner; with such an one no not to eat. Know ye not that the unrighteous shall not inherit the kingdom of God? Be not deceived: neither fornicators, nor idolaters, nor adulterers, nor effeminate, nor abusers of themselves with humankind, will inherit the Kingdom of God… Do you not know that your bodies are members of Christ himself? Shall I then take the members of Christ and unite them with a prostitute? Never! Do you not know that he who unites himself with a prostitute is one with her in body? For it is said, The two will become one flesh. But whoever is united with the Lord is one with him in spirit." (1 Corinthians 5:11–12, 6:9, 15–19 KJV)

"Put to death, therefore, whatever belongs to your earthly nature: sexual immorality, impurity, lust, evil desires and greed, which is idolatry. Because of these, the wrath of God is coming. You used to walk in these ways, in the life you once lived. But now you must also rid yourselves of all such things as these: anger, rage, malice, slander, and filthy language from your lips. Do not lie to each other, since you have taken off your old self with its practices and have put on the new self, which is being renewed in knowledge in the image of its Creator. Here there is no Gentile or Jew, circumcised or uncircumcised, barbarian, Scythian, slave or free, but Christ is all, and is in all. Therefore, as God's chosen people, holy and dearly loved, clothe yourselves with compassion, kindness, humility, gentleness and patience. Bear with each other and forgive one another if any of you has a grievance against someone. Forgive as the Lord forgave you. And over all these virtues put on love, which binds them all together in perfect unity." (Colossians 3:5–14, Ephesians 4:29)

"But among you there must not be even a hint of sexual immorality, or of any kind of impurity, or of greed, because these are improper for God's holy people. Nor should there be obscenity, foolish talk or coarse joking, which are out of place, but rather thanksgiving. For of this you can be sure: No immoral, impure or greedy person—such a person is an idolater—has any inheritance in the kingdom of Christ and of God. Let no one deceive you with empty words, for because of such things God's wrath comes on those who are disobedient. Therefore do not be partners with them." (Ephesians 5:3–7)

"Children, obey your parents in the Lord: for this is right. Honor your father and mother which is the first commandment with promise." (Ephesians 6:1–2)

"Slaves, obey your earthly masters in everything; and do it, not only when their eye is on you and to curry their favor, but with sincerity of heart and reverence for the Lord. Whatever you do, work at it with all your heart, as working for the Lord, not for human masters." (Colossians 3:21–23)

"Let everyone be subject to the governing authorities, for there is no authority except that which God has established. The authorities that exist have been established by God. Consequently, whoever rebels against the authority is rebelling against what God has instituted, and those who do so will bring judgment on themselves." (Romans 13:1–7)

"It is God's will that you should be sanctified: that you should avoid sexual immorality; that each of you should learn to control your own body in a way that is holy and honorable, not in passionate lust like the pagans, who do not know God; and that in this matter no one should wrong or take advantage of a brother or sister. The Lord will punish all those who commit such sins, as we told you and warned you before. For God did not call us to be impure, but to live a holy life. Therefore, anyone who rejects this instruction does not reject a human being but God, the very God who gives you his Holy Spirit." (1 Thessalonians 4:3–8)

"Brothers and sisters, if someone is caught in a sin, you who live by the Spirit should restore that person gently. But watch yourselves, or you also may be tempted. Carry each other's burdens, and in this way you will fulfill the law of Christ. If anyone thinks they are something when they are not, they deceive themselves. Do nothing out of selfish ambition or vain conceit. Rather, in humility value others above yourselves, not looking to your own interests but each of you to the interests of the others." (Galatians 6:2, Philippians 2:3-4)

"But godliness with contentment is great gain. For we brought nothing into the world, and we can take nothing out of it. But if we have food and clothing, we will be content with that. Those who want to get rich fall into temptation and a trap and into many foolish and harmful desires that plunge people into ruin and destruction. For the love of money is a root of all kinds of evil. Some people, eager for money, have wandered from the faith and pierced themselves with many griefs." (1 Timothy 6:6–10)

"Has not God chosen those who are poor in the eyes of the world to be rich in faith and to inherit the kingdom he promised those who love him?" (James 2:5)

"Therefore, since we are receiving a kingdom that cannot be shaken, let us be thankful, and so worship God acceptably with reverence and awe." (Hebrews 12:28)

"Be thankful in all circumstances because this is God's will for you in Christ Jesus." (1 Thessalonians 5:18)

"Devote yourselves to prayer, being watchful and thankful." (Colossians 4:2)

"Now we ask you, brothers and sisters, to acknowledge those who work hard among you, who care for you in the Lord and who admonish you. Hold them in the highest regard in love because of their work. Live in peace with each other. And we urge you, brothers and sisters, warn those who are idle and disruptive, encourage the disheartened, help the weak, be patient with everyone. Make sure that nobody pays back wrong for wrong, but always strive to do what is good for each other and for everyone else. Rejoice always, pray continually, give thanks in all circumstances; for this is God's will for you in Christ Jesus."(1 Thessalonians 5:12–16)

"And we know that in all things God works for the good of those who love him, who have been called according to his purpose." (Romans 8:28) (That must have been difficult to absorb if you were being fed to the lions in the arenas or crucified for your belief in Christ.)

"Do not take revenge, my dear friends, but leave room for God's wrath, for it is written: It is mine to avenge; I will repay, says the Lord. On the contrary: If your enemy is hungry, feed him; if he is thirsty, give him something to drink. In doing this, you will heap burning coals on his head." (Romans 12:20, Proverbs 25:21–22) Jesus said to love your enemies without equivocation [Matthew 5:44, Luke 6:27–30].) *Note: There seems to be a little ulterior motive here. Jesus said to love your enemies without equivocation.* (Matthew 5:44, Luke 6:27-30)

"Finally, brothers and sisters, whatever is true, whatever is noble, whatever is right, whatever is pure, whatever is lovely, whatever is admirable—if anything is excellent or praiseworthy—think about such things." (Philippians 4:8)

Appendix C

The Nicene Creed

We believe in one God,
the Father, the Almighty,
maker of heaven and earth,
of all that is, seen and unseen.

We believe in one Lord, Jesus Christ,
the only Son of God,
eternally begotten of the Father,
God from God, Light from Light,
true God from true God,
begotten, not made,
of one Being with the Father.
Through him all things were made.
For us and for our salvation
he came down from heaven:
by the power of the Holy Spirit
he became incarnate from the Virgin Mary,
and was made man.
For our sake he was crucified under Pontius Pilate;
he suffered death and was buried.
On the third day he rose again
in accordance with the Scriptures;
he ascended into heaven

and is seated at the right hand of the Father.
He will come again in glory to judge the living and the dead,
and his kingdom will have no end.

We believe in the Holy Spirit, the Lord, the giver of life,
who proceeds from the Father and the Son.
With the Father and the Son he is worshiped and glorified.
He has spoken through the Prophets.
We believe in one holy catholic and apostolic Church.
We acknowledge one baptism for the forgiveness of sins.
We look for the resurrection of the dead,
and the life of the world to come. Amen.

Appendix D

How the Myers-Briggs Type Indicator Applies to Christian Faith

(https://www.gotquestions.org/Myers-Briggs-Type-Indicator.html, reprinted under fair use doctrine for education from *Christian Counseling, 2006* by Gary Collins)

The Myers-Briggs Type Indicator (MBTI) is a popular personality inventory based on Dr. Carl G. Jung's theory of psychological types. The test was developed by Isabel Briggs Myers and her mother, Katharine Briggs, to help people understand themselves and each other better. It was adopted as a professional psychological assessment in 1975 by CPP Inc. It has proven to be very popular and offers a very effective method of using personality theory in church populations. Whether or not people have taken the official psychological assessment, many have heard of the terms and have unofficially tested their personalities or self-identified with a specific type. Descriptions abound of applications for personality traits, strengths, and weaknesses, preferred jobs for each type, best learning environments for each type, leadership, and team building, and even romantic combinations of each type. It also has been investigated extensively for application with religious and spirituality aspects of human behavior. (The MBTI applies only to normal behaviors and does not apply to any personality disorders or mental illness. Consult a professional for diagnosis and treatment of such malfunctions.)

The MBTI selects preferences in four different psychological functions and specifies sixteen personality types. The emphasis is on preferences and not skills or ability. The areas of preference include (1) a focus on energy either from the exterior world (extroversion, *E*) or the interior world (introversion, *I*); (2) a focus on perceiving the world through observable information (sensing, *S*) or interpreting and anticipating future events (intuition, *I*); (3) making decisions by first looking at logical reasoning (thinking, *T*) or by first considering the people involved and their concerns (feeling, *F*); and (4) a desire for things to be decided and settled using thinking or feeling (judging, *J*) or being open to other options using sensing or intuition (perceiving, *P*).

The combinations of those four preferences describes sixteen personality types. For example, *ISTJ* is a personality type that is basically introverted, focused on sensory information, logical reasoning, and most comfortable when decision making has been resolved. ENFP is extraverted and prefers intuition and feelings and keeping options open while introversion, sensing, thinking and deciding are less important. This book is a product of my personality type, INTJ, that is, introverted, intuitive, thinking, judging, with extraversion, sensing, feeling, and openness having less importance. Research indicates that women tend more to prefer feeling and men tend more to prefer thinking—which helps to explain a lot of the communications issues between genders.

A well-developed personality has access to all four of the functions, but not equally. The primary function will drive behavior with the others providing support and maintenance as needed. Perhaps you can imagine how people with various personalities may experience the dynamics in church groups—including worship services. To provide fullness for all personality types, the church experience must appeal to the sensing and intuition functions as well as the thinking and feeling functions. Of these, it may be the intuition function that opens into the spirit, as Jung claimed it can "see around corners." Faith is defined as "confidence in what we hope for and assurance about what we do not see" (Hebrews 11:1). People may learn to behave in certain ways in school, family, work, or church, for the benefits achieved, but their preferred personality functions stay pretty much the same throughout their lives. However, it is possible to learn to engage all four functions—sensing, intuition, thinking, and feeling with some desire and practice.

The Myers & Briggs Foundation is careful to point out that no one personality type is better than any other personality type. Also, personality types are not indicative of ability or character. The type descriptions simply are offered as helpful tools in better understanding oneself and increasing tolerance for others. Personality-type preference might be helpful in making life choices, but it should not be the only tool a person uses to determine career path, romantic partners, or religious practice. Our bodies change as we age and we can learn to change behavior, but the preferred personality stays pretty much the same. However, when people are stressed as from a family emergency, loss of a loved one, or natural disaster, they may exhibit symptoms of posttrauma shock or depression by acting abnormally, which should be referred to a qualified counselor. If people obviously acting distressed do not ask for help, perhaps the pastor can respectfully offer to meet privately for discussion.

The secular scientific considerations of the MBTI notwithstanding, is the idea that there are different personality types biblical? Are personality types something Christians should consider? Are they helpful in any way? Do people employ their personality types in matters of spirituality? Can the church use the MBTI for better organizing and service of its members? Yes. The functions of personality—sensing, intuition, thinking, and feeling—may be subtle and difficult to discern, but they drive behaviors, opinions, and relationships in very powerful ways. Churches must conduct "ministries" that appeal to all four personality functions—sensory, intellectual, emotional, and spiritual to feed the needs of everyone in the flock. This is a difficult task for sure, but often it is worth developing.

We know that all humans are made in the image of God (Genesis 1:27). But no two human beings are made exactly the same, and God would have to be both male and female—but God always is referred to in the masculine, he/him. We know that we are uniquely formed and that God fully knows us and fully loves us (Psalm 139).

Nothing in the MBTI contradicts this as people of the same type are uniquely different. Simple observation tells us that some people seem energized by spending time with others whereas other people recharge best alone, that is, extraverts and introverts respectively. The Bible leaves room for there being different types of people as well as for commonalities among the different types in churches. The fact that John/Jane Doe is unique does not mean that every single thing is different from everyone else. Just as human bodies are different but similar, so are their personalities.

The benefit of the MBTI for Christians is in helping us better understand ourselves to better serve God in our own ways. Often, our personality traits coincide with God's call on our lives. For example, we might tend more toward introversion and have as part of our call being a writer. Or perhaps we tend more toward extroversion and find that God has asked us to host group Bible studies. Knowing our "natural" strengths can help us be attuned to the places where we can serve most effectively, knowing our "natural" weaknesses might help us avoid calls for service that would more easily trip us up and possibly cause undue stress.

Understanding personality types also can help Christians better love and serve others who behave differently. For example, when we know that one of our friends tends more toward introversion, we'll know that time spent together one on one is probably more meaningful than time spent together in larger social settings. If our friend tends more toward extroversion, we'll know that he enjoys being included in social activities, so we can be sure to invite him to share or lead group meetings. Understanding personality types also can help us more easily accept differing behavior of others. For instance, when an introverted friend says "no thanks" to our invitation to a get-together, we might not take it as personally. Or when a person who is a "thinker" talks first about the bottom line in a church budget, we can recognize that his words are not due to hard-heartedness but to the way God has naturally wired him for information analysis. When a "feeler" invokes the interest of people in decision making, it may pay to listen. If a person has difficulty coming to a conclusion, we can see his desire for perception, sensing or intuition, outweighs his desire for judging—thinking or feeling. On the other hand, if a person tends to jump to conclusions, they can work around the desire for judging and help to balance it with more perception. No one behaves in church, as in the world, exactly as any other person. If church leaders understand these aspects of personality, they can organize people, conduct meetings, and arrange activities for better results.

One danger of the MBTI for Christians, or for anyone, is in making personality type inflexible and using it to justify disruptive behavior. One's personality type does not excuse bad behavior, nor does it limit one's ability to act differently or to do (and enjoy) things not stereotypically within the type. An introvert is still called to share the Gospel. An extrovert is still called to spend time alone with God. A thinker should still consider how his decisions may affect other people. A feeler is still expected to be a good steward. When God calls us outside of our comfort zone, personality type is not a reason to resist because all growth requires some suffering. Since no one, save Jesus, volunteers for suffering, perhaps it is forced upon us to provide the growth that only comes from suffering. We are given problems to learn how to solve problems. If anything, a call of God that challenges our natural inclinations gives us more opportunity to trust him and a deeper understanding that it is only his work in us that causes amazing things to be accomplished (Zechariah 4:6). The Holy Spirit provides many ways for people of different personality types to serve God through serving others.

(Apostle Paul realized this principle when he described the church as the body of Christ, which, like a human body, has various parts each of which are necessary to make up the whole so that no one part should boast or claim superiority—except maybe the brain, which seems to control all the rest [Romans 12:5–8, 1 Corinthians 12:27]. I [INTJ] was a Sunday school teacher and deacon and my late wife, who was a preacher's daughter [ENFP], led a drama program, played piano and organ, and served in women's missionary work. I much prefer solitary time in meditation and writing instead of group activities.)

Another danger of the MBTI is in allowing it to define the totality of our identities. A Christian is first and foremost a child of God (John 1:12). Our personality is something God designed, and it is certainly something to explore so that we can develop more fully as human beings. Happiness comes from losing ourselves in service to others. But we are defined first by faith in Jesus and the call to his church. Paul was willing to lose all things "that I may gain Christ and be found in him, not having a righteousness of my own…but that which is through faith in Christ" (Philippians 3:8–9).

The Myers-Briggs Type Indicator (MBTI) can be a helpful tool in understanding God's unique design of humanity and of yourself specifically. It hints at both the order and diversity with which God created the world, demonstrating his logic and his artistry. Understanding ourselves and others can help us better employ the gifts God has provided. Rather than try to become someone different, we can thank God for his unique design and make the best use of the gifts God has given us for his service while encouraging and accepting the contribution of others to the body of Christ. Church leaders would do well to engage a professional MBTI counselor to help implement it with their congregations. To locate a qualified counselor, visit www.apt.org and for help in understanding your personality type visit www.mbtionline.com, www.16personalities.com, www.humanmetrics.com, and www.personalitypage.com. If you know your four-letter type code, you can find many descriptions by browsing it on the internet. All in God's will, of course.

Appendix E

My Favorite Hymn

Christianity has motivated the creation of great art, architecture, poetry, drama, and music throughout the centuries. Some people find participation and observations of God's creation through such human expressions to be a wonderful connection to the Supreme Being. I like music, and many of the traditional hymns transport me into the "closer walk with thee." Here are lyrics for the hymn I would select as my favorite. Perhaps you can add some others to your own private collection.

In the Garden

I come to the garden alone
While the dew is still on the roses
And the voice I hear, falling on my ear
The Son of God discloses

He speaks and the sound of His voice
Is so sweet the birds hush their singing
And the melody that he gave to me
Within my heart is ringing

And he walks with me
And He talks with me
And He tells me I am His own
And the joy we share as we tarry there
None other has ever known

Songwriter: C. Austin Miles
© Warner/Chappell Music, Inc., Kobalt Music Publishing Ltd.,

Recommended Resources

Books

Holy Bible, New International Version®, NIV® Copyright ©1973, 1978, 1984, 2011 by Biblica, Inc.® *Used by permission. All rights reserved worldwide.*

Aquilina, Mike. *The Fathers of the Church. Expanded Edition.* Our Sunday Visitor, 2006.

Barker, Dan. *Free Will Explained: How Science and Philosophy Converged to Produce a Beautiful Illusion*, Sterling, 2018.

Barker, Dan. *God, the Most Unpleasant Character in All Fiction*, Sterling Reprint Edition, 2018.

Borg, Marcus J. *The Heart of Christianity – Rediscovering a Life of Faith*, HarperOne, 2015.

Collins, Gary. *Christian Counseling. Third Edition.* Thomas Nelson, Inc., 2006.

Conner, David Jonah. *All That's Wrong With the Bible.* 2017.

Felten, David and Procter-Murphy, Jeff. *Living the Questions: The Wisdom of Progressive Christianity,* HarperCollins, 2012.

Geisler, Norman L. *Christian Apologetics.* Baker Academic, 2013.

Harbaugh, Gary L. *God's Gifted People*, Augsburg Fortress, 1991.

Price, Robert M. *The Pre-Nicene New Testament*, Signature Books, 2006.

Price, Robert M. *The Christ Myth Theory and Its Problems*, American Atheist Press, 2011.

Price, Robert M. *Bart Ehrman Interpreted*, Pitchstone Publishing, 2018.

Price, Robert M. *Paperback Apocalypse: How the Christian Church Was Left Behind,* Prometheus Books, 2007.

Reeves, Ryan Matthew and Hill, Charles. *Know How We Got Our Bible*, 2018.
Shermer, Michael. *Skeptic, Viewing the World With a Rational Eye*, St. Martens Griffin, 2017.
Shermer, Michael. *Heavens on Earth, the Scientific Search for the Afterlife, Immortality and Utopia*, Henry Holt & Co., 2018.
Shermer, Michael. *How We Believe: Science, Skepticism and the Search for God*. Holt Paperbacks, 2003.
Spong, John Shelby. *Unbelievable – Why Neither Ancient Creeds Nor the Reformation Can Produce a Living Faith Today*. HarperOne, 2018.
Tagliaferre, Lewis. *A Labyrinth Walk of Life*. Christian Faith Publishing, 2018.
Thielen, Martin. *What's the Least I Can Believe and Still Be a Christian*, West Minster John Knox, 2013.
Thompson, Frank Charles. *The New Chain Reference Bible, Third Improved Edition*, B.B. Kirkbride Bible Co., Inc. 1934–2016.
Yalom, Irvin D. *Staring at the Sun – Overcoming the Terror of Death*. Jossey-Bass, 2009.

Web Sites

www.betterlivingbetterdying.com
www.essentialchristianity.com
www.finalexitnetwork.org
www.humanmetrics.com
www.myersbriggs.org
www.mbtionline.com
www.nccih.nih.gov
www.16personalities.com
www.selfdevelopment.com
www.seventhelementliving.com
www.thelawofattraction.com
www.theurapeutictouch.org

About the Author

The author provides this book as the completion of a series of books which, at his age of eighty-five years, document his personal search for inner peace after many challenges, losses, and some success. After service on a B-36 bomber crew in the U.S. Force during the Korean War, he was educated in engineering and business. He published a technical journal for twenty-seven years and wrote dozens of magazine articles on electricity and energy policy, plus several books on his personal philosophy of life. He was married to a preacher's daughter (deceased) and raised two children. After being a church deacon and Sunday School teacher, his self-development led to discovery of Theofatalism. His other book titles are: Recovery from Loss, Kisses aren't Contracts, Voices of Sedona, Baby Boomer Lamentations, Theofatalism, A Labyrinth Walk of Life, Creating Serenity in Chaos, and Better Living, Better Dying. However, it is not about the author, it is about the message. The author merely was the scribe who was given the message to sow as seeds thrown among the grains of sand on the desert of human suffering. Some of them will be blown away, some will rot and decay, and a few seeds may take root and grow to produce new seeds, and so it will be. All in God's will of course.

CPSIA information can be obtained
at www.ICGtesting.com
Printed in the USA
FFHW020226071119
55997877-61848FF

9 781644 920206